Beyond Tomorrow

The Future of AI and Humanity

by
Riley S. Ashton

Beyond Tomorrow

The Future of AI and Humanity

Contents

Introduction 1

Chapter 1: Understanding AI Today 4

    The Foundations of AI.. 4

    Current Applications of AI.. 7

Chapter 2: The Evolution of AI Technology 11

    Key Milestones in AI Development..................................... 12

    Breakthroughs Shaping the Future 14

Chapter 3: The Societal Impact of AI 19

    AI and the Workforce Transformation 19

    Shifting Cultural Norms 22

Chapter 4: AI in Healthcare 26

    Innovations in Medical Diagnosis 26

    Ethical Implications in Healthcare AI 29

Chapter 5: AI and Education 33

    Personalized Learning Experiences 33

    Educator Roles in an AI-Driven World............................... 36

Chapter 6: Ethical Considerations of AI................................ 40

    Developing AI Ethics Frameworks 40

    The Debate on AI Rights.. 44

Chapter 7: AI in Governance and Policy 48

    Shaping AI Legislation 49

    Government Use of AI Technologies.................................... 52

Chapter 8: AI and the Environment 55

    AI in Climate Change Mitigation.. 55

Sustainability Challenges and Opportunities................................58

Chapter 9: Autonomous Systems and Robotics 62

    Advances in Autonomous Technology......................................63

    The Future of Human-Robot Interaction 65

Chapter 10: AI in Arts and Creativity..69

    AI as a Collaborative Partner 69

    Redefining Artistic Boundaries..72

Chapter 11: AI and Human Relationships...76

    The Evolution of Communication..76

    Impacts on Social Dynamics 79

Chapter 12: AI and Security 83

    Cybersecurity Threats and Solutions..83

    AI in National Defense...86

Chapter 13: The Future of AI in Business 90

    Transforming Business Models...90

    AI and Customer Experiences..93

Chapter 14: Global Perspectives on AI 97

    AI Adoption Across Nations 97

    International Collaboration and Competition 101

Chapter 15: Moral and Philosophical Questions 104

    AI and Consciousness Debate...105

    The Human Element in AI Development 107

Chapter 16: The Economics of AI 111

    AI and Economic Disparities 111

    Reshaping Global Markets...114

Chapter 17: Privacy in an AI World..117

    Balancing Innovation and Privacy 117

    Implications for Personal Data 120

Chapter 18: AI in Transportation...124

    The Rise of Autonomous Vehicles..124

AI-Driven Transportation Innovations 127

Chapter 19: AI and Augmented Reality 131

Enhancing Perceptions with AI 132

Integrating AI in Virtual Spaces 134

Chapter 20: Preparing the Next Generation 138

Education for an AI-Driven Future 138

Cultivating Future-Proof Skills 141

Chapter 21: AI Ethics and Responsibility 145

Accountability in AI Design 145

Implementing Responsible AI Practices 149

Chapter 22: Visionaries and Thought Leaders 152

Perspectives Shaping AI's Future 152

Influencers in AI Innovation 155

Chapter 23: The Limits of AI 158

Understanding AI's Capabilities 158

Boundaries Yet to Be Overcome 161

Chapter 24: Living in Harmony with AI 165

Navigating Coexistence with Technology 165

Collaborative Futures with AI 168

Chapter 25: Imagining AI 50 Years From Now 172

Predictions and Projections 173

Preparing for Uncertain Changes 175

Conclusion 179

Appendix A: Appendix 182

1. Further Reading and Resources 182

2. Glossary of Terms 183

3. Ethical Guidelines 183

4. Frequently Asked Questions 183

Introduction

In a rapidly evolving world where technology shapes the very fabric of our society, few advancements stand as poised for transformative impact as artificial intelligence. From its humble beginnings in research laboratories, AI has burgeoned into an all-encompassing force, influencing aspects of life we once thought to be uniquely human. As we embark on this journey through the future of AI, the aim is not only to understand how this powerful tool will shape our tomorrow but to spark a dialogue on the complex intersection of technology, ethics, and humanity.

Today, the reach of AI extends far beyond the technological sector. It permeates healthcare, education, governance, and even art, challenging our perceptions of what machines can achieve. As automation accelerates, we're standing on the precipice of a new era, one with both profound opportunities and daunting challenges. AI's potential to revolutionize industries, create new economic models, and redefine societal norms is immense. Yet, it also calls into question our preparedness as a society to harness its extraordinary capabilities responsibly.

The evolution of AI technology is not a linear narrative but rather a tapestry of breakthroughs and setbacks. Over the decades, research in AI has ebbed and flowed, driven by technological progress and tempered by limitations in understanding and implementation. Each milestone in AI's journey underscores the relentless pursuit to create machines that can think, learn, and potentially surpass human intelligence. As we delve into the current state and future possibilities of AI, we need to explore both its potential to improve lives and the ethical considerations it demands.

While AI has demonstrated a remarkable ability to transform data into insights, decisions, and personalized experiences, the societal implications cannot be understated. AI is reshaping our world—bringing efficiencies yet altering job landscapes, personal privacy, and global power dynamics. The dialogue surrounding AI is not merely about its technological viability but also about its cultural, ethical, and social impact.

One of the primary concerns is how AI will redefine the workforce. With automation encroaching upon both routine and complex tasks, industries must adapt to the reality of a transformed labor market. The potential for AI to enhance productivity and innovation is unparalleled, but it also brings significant challenges. Societies must grapple with questions of employment, income distribution, and the very nature of work, ensuring that the benefits of AI advancements are accessible to all.

AI's influence extends into education, promising personalized learning experiences that cater to the unique needs of each student. Yet, it also requires us to reconsider the role of educators in an AI-driven world. Teachers are no longer just dispensers of knowledge but facilitators of critical thinking and creativity. Their role evolves into guiding students in navigating an increasingly complex technological landscape. Equipping the next generation with the skills necessary to thrive in an AI-enhanced world is paramount.

Moreover, the integration of AI into governance and policy formulation is inevitable. As governments explore AI's potential for improving public services, they also bear the immense responsibility of shaping legislation that protects citizens' rights and freedoms. Thoughtful consideration must be given to the ethical frameworks guiding AI development, balancing innovation with societal well-being and privacy concerns.

We're also witnessing AI's foray into creative domains, challenging the boundaries of human artistry. AI can collaborate with artists to create new forms of expression, blurring the lines between human creativity and machine-generated art. This collaboration prompts a reevaluation of copyrights, artistic ownership, and the appreciation of digitally created works.

The ethical landscape of AI is complex and multifaceted. As we push the boundaries of what AI can do, we must remain vigilant in our pursuit of ethical AI frameworks. The debate on AI rights, accountability, and governance is critical in ensuring that these technologies serve humanity's best interests rather than succumb to unintended harms.

Looking forward, imagining AI fifty years from now elicits both excitement and caution. Our challenge is to foresee the trajectory of AI advancements, anticipate the shift in societal norms, and prepare for uncertainties. By fostering a comprehensive understanding of AI's potential and its limitations, we can better navigate the future, ensuring that technology enhances, rather than detracts from, the human experience.

This book endeavors to guide you through the complex landscape of AI's future. It's an exploration filled with possibility, underpinned by the responsibility we must accept in shaping a future that harmonizes technological innovation with ethical stewardship. As we journey together, let us embrace the potential of AI to create a better, more equitable world for everyone.

Chapter 1:
Understanding AI Today

Artificial intelligence (AI) has seamlessly integrated into the fabric of our daily lives, subtly transforming how we interact with technology and each other. It's a dynamic field, rooted in mathematical algorithms and powered by data, capable of learning, reasoning, and self-correction. Today's AI technologies are shaping industries by driving innovation and efficiency, from enhancing customer service through chatbots to optimizing supply chain logistics and improving medical diagnostics. However, AI's current applications only scratch the surface of its potential, leaving us both intrigued and concerned about the future this powerful tool could create. As we navigate these transformative times, understanding the foundations, limitations, and ethical implications of AI becomes vital for ensuring that its development aligns with the broader goals of society. By recognizing AI's potential and embracing its complexities, we can channel its capabilities to improve the human experience in ways previously unimagined.

The Foundations of AI

Over the past few decades, artificial intelligence has transformed from a futuristic concept into a daily reality that shapes the world around us. But to truly understand its impact and potential, we have to look back at its roots, where theoretical underpinnings and pioneering work laid the foundation for modern AI. These origins fuel not only technological advances but also philosophical and ethical debates that are more pertinent than ever.

The intellectual groundwork for AI can be traced back to ancient times, where myths and stories spoke of automatons and intelligent machines. Fast-forward to the mid-20th century, and you encounter the formative years of AI as a scientific discipline. Figures like Alan Turing started asking fundamental questions: Can machines think? Turing's seminal 1950 paper, "Computing Machinery and Intelligence," introduced what's now known as the Turing Test, a milestone that continues to provoke discussion about machine capability and consciousness.

Though early AI research was primarily theoretical, its aspirations were grand. The Dartmouth Conference in 1956, chaired by John McCarthy, Marvin Minsky, Nathaniel Rochester, and Claude Shannon, is widely recognized as the birth of organized AI research. It laid out ambitious goals to simulate intellectual processes characteristic of human beings. By proposing to explore what's possible through computers, the conference essentially set the stage for AI as a formal field of study.

These formative events weren't just about dreaming big; they generated concrete approaches to creating intelligent systems. Logic programming, neural networks, and heuristic algorithms became focal points in early AI development. While today's researchers have transcended many rudimentary systems of the past, these initial frameworks still serve as the backbone for contemporary technologies. For instance, neural networks—once constrained by limited computational power—have evolved into deep learning techniques that fuel today's innovations in image and speech recognition.

However, AI's journey has been anything but linear. Over the past several decades, it has experienced several 'AI winters,' periods marked by disillusionment and reduced funding, usually due to unmet expectations and technical limitations. But these setbacks were crucial, prompting the community to reevaluate goals and methods. They led to tremendous innovation, from expert systems in the '80s to more recent advancements like unsupervised learning.

One of the key philosophical debates underpinning AI from its inception revolves around the concept of intelligence. What does it mean for a machine to be 'intelligent'? Does mastering a particular task reflect intelligence, or is there a qualitative difference between human and artificial thought processes? The discussion has profound implications, influencing everything from development models to ethical guidelines. This focus on intelligence drives current research into emulating not just human tasks but aspects of our emotional and social intelligence as well.

Understanding AI's foundations also necessitates a look at its ethical and societal considerations. As AI systems become more integrated into society, issues such as bias, privacy, and employment gradually took the main stage, transforming from speculative concerns into urgent public policy questions. Initially, these issues might have seemed abstract or distant, but developments over the last few years have shown us how AI can magnify societal inequities if unchecked.

The ethical implications inform not just what AI can do but what it should do. Early pioneers couldn't possibly anticipate every responsibility AI would inherit, making ethical frameworks a continuous and complex area of study. Regulatory bodies worldwide are beginning to develop guidelines and standards aimed at ensuring AI technologies remain beneficial to humanity. These aren't just bureaucratic measures; they're informed by the philosophical and theoretical roots of AI itself, guiding our collective approach toward technological stewardship.

Another pioneering element of AI's foundation is collaboration across disparate scientific disciplines. AI thrives at the intersection of computer science, mathematics, neuroscience, and even sociology. This multidisciplinary environment has proven indispensable, cultivating innovation through cross-pollination of ideas and methodologies. Researchers aren't just building better algorithms; they're decoding the complexities of perception, decision-making, and adaptation, which fuel both AI's progress and its profound impact on society.

In today's AI landscape, rediscovering these foundational theories and approaches can catalyze modern breakthroughs. Looking back offers a roadmap for navigating what lies ahead—an odyssey that involves not just technical advancements but ethical maturity and social responsibility. As AI continues to grow and evolve, its foundational principles remain a touchstone, reminding us that while technology may shape the future, it is people who should guide its direction.

Current Applications of AI

Artificial intelligence has swiftly permeated numerous facets of contemporary life, manifesting in diverse applications that stretch across varied domains. From enhancing daily conveniences to revolutionizing major industries, AI's scope continues to expand at a rapid pace. In this chapter, we delve into some of the current applications of AI that demonstrate its transformative potential and influence on society today.

One of the most visible applications of AI is its use in personal digital assistants like Siri, Alexa, and Google Assistant. These AI-driven platforms have become integral to countless households, offering users improved convenience in managing daily tasks. Through the seamless integration of voice recognition and natural language processing, these assistants can execute commands, provide information, and control smart home devices, essentially reshaping how we interact with technology on a personal level.

AI's impact extends beyond personal convenience. In the realm of healthcare, machine learning algorithms facilitate early diagnosis and treatment. AI systems analyze medical images, such as MRIs and X-rays, with remarkable accuracy, often surpassing human performance. This capability is critical in fields where early detection can significantly improve outcomes, such as oncology and cardiology. AI also supports personalized medicine by analyzing genetic data to tailor treatments to individual patients, potentially improving therapeutic effectiveness and reducing side effects.

In the retail industry, AI enhances the shopping experience through personalized recommendations and optimized supply chains. Retail giants use AI algorithms to analyze consumer behavior and preferences, curating bespoke suggestions that increase customer satisfaction and sales. Additionally, AI-powered inventory management systems predict demand trends, helping businesses maintain optimal stock levels while minimizing waste and storage costs.

The finance sector has also embraced AI, utilizing algorithms for fraud detection, risk assessment, and automated trading. By scrutinizing vast datasets for unusual patterns, AI systems can swiftly identify and respond to potential threats. Automated trading bots run by AI can analyze market conditions and execute trades at lightning speed, contributing to the efficiency and fluidity of financial markets.

Transportation is yet another domain experiencing significant changes due to AI. Autonomous vehicles, driven by sophisticated AI algorithms, are no longer confined to the realm of science fiction. Companies like Tesla and Waymo are testing self-driving cars and trucks, aiming to enhance road safety and offer new mobility solutions. AI in transportation extends beyond vehicles; it also optimizes logistics and supply chains, improving the efficiency of delivery systems worldwide.

In the entertainment industry, AI has taken on roles as creators and collaborators. Algorithms can compose music, write scripts, and even generate artwork, challenging traditional notions of authorship and creativity. Music recommendation services like Spotify and video streaming platforms such as Netflix use AI to understand user tastes and suggest content, thus transforming the way audiences consume media.

Education systems are progressively incorporating AI to offer personalized learning experiences. AI tutors and learning platforms adapt to individual student needs, offering tailored lessons that nurture student potential and promote engagement. By analyzing data on performance and learning styles, AI can support educators in crafting highly effective educational strategies.

Agriculture benefits from AI through precision farming techniques that optimize crop yields and resource usage. AI-driven drones and sensors gather data on soil and weather conditions, enabling farmers to make informed decisions and improve productivity. These innovations not only bolster food production but also support sustainable practices by reducing the consumption of water, fertilizers, and pesticides.

AI is making strides in art and fashion as well, spawning new creative processes and designs. Designers use AI to explore innovative patterns and materials, pushing the boundaries of what is possible in the creative industries. As AI models evolve, they collaborate with human creators to develop unique and captivating products that reflect a blend of human intuition and machine learning.

Sports and athletics also stand to gain from AI's analytical prowess. AI tools offer insights into player performance and game strategies, providing teams with a competitive edge. By analyzing data from numerous games and conditions, AI can predict outcomes and optimize training regimens to enhance athlete performance.

Finally, AI plays a crucial role in addressing environmental challenges. AI models predict climate patterns, inform conservation efforts, and contribute to sustainable energy solutions. By processing vast ecological datasets, AI systems help scientists and policymakers devise effective strategies to combat climate change and protect biodiversity.

Although the current applications of AI are remarkable, the future holds even greater promise. As technologies continue to develop, AI's influence on industries and our daily lives will likely deepen, bringing with it new opportunities and challenges. Navigating these changes will require thoughtful consideration and innovative approaches to ensure AI remains a positive force in our evolving world.

Chapter 2:
The Evolution of AI Technology

O ver the decades, the journey of artificial intelligence has presented a tapestry of breakthroughs and hurdles, reflecting the spirit of human ingenuity and resilience. From its humble beginnings, AI has evolved into a multifaceted powerhouse that now shapes many facets of our daily lives, nurturing both the excitement of possibility and the caution of unforeseen consequences. Milestones such as machine learning algorithms and deep learning have acted as catalysts for AI's transformation, pushing the boundaries of what machines can achieve. As we stand at the frontier of this technological evolution, it's clear that the rapid pace of development holds profound implications for our future. The promise of AI isn't just in its ability to streamline tasks or optimize processes but in its potential to redefine how we interact with the world around us. As we navigate these transformative times, understanding AI's evolution becomes essential for leveraging its benefits while addressing the challenges it poses. The tapestry of AI's history is as much about the triumphs yet to come as it is about the innovations that have brought us to this pivotal moment. Exploring this evolution not only grounds us in what has been achieved but also ignites the imagination for what lies ahead in the relentless march of progress.

Key Milestones in AI Development

Artificial intelligence, a concept that once seemed confined to science fiction, has now become an integral part of our daily lives. The journey of AI's evolution is marked by various key milestones that have shaped its development. Each milestone represents not just an academic or technological breakthrough but also shifts in societal and economic paradigms.

AI's history can be traced back to the mid-20th century when British mathematician Alan Turing laid the groundwork with his seminal 1950 paper "Computing Machinery and Intelligence." In it, he proposed what is now known as the Turing Test, a measure of a machine's ability to exhibit intelligent behavior indistinguishable from a human. This idea was foundational, setting off a quest to develop machines capable of "thinking."

The 1956 Dartmouth Conference, often considered the birthplace of AI as an academic discipline, brought together visionaries like John McCarthy and Marvin Minsky. These pioneers coined the term "artificial intelligence" and set ambitious goals, envisioning that machines would match human intelligence soon. Despite their optimism, progress was slower than anticipated. Challenges like limited processing power and the complexity of human cognition led to periods known as "AI winters," where funding and interest waned.

Despite the setbacks, the 1980s saw renewed interest in AI with the advent of expert systems. These were programs designed to mimic the decision-making abilities of a human expert in specific fields such as medical diagnosis or geological exploration. Expert systems showcased AI's potential to assist in complex problem-solving, leading to increased commercial interest and investment in AI research and development.

The 1990s and early 2000s marked a shift towards practical applications of AI, fueled by advancements in computational power and data availability. IBM's Deep Blue famously defeated world chess champion Garry Kasparov in 1997, demonstrating AI's capability in processing complex game strategies beyond human limits. This victory had profound implications, not just in gaming but in illustrating the potential for AI to tackle highly structured problem domains.

The advent of the internet and the digital revolution provided vast amounts of data, a crucial ingredient that propelled AI toward machine learning. The development of neural networks, particularly deep learning models inspired by the human brain's structure, represented a major leap forward. In 2012, a deep learning algorithm achieved unprecedented accuracy in an image classification challenge, signaling a new era of AI capabilities.

Google's acquisition of DeepMind in 2014 marked another significant milestone. DeepMind's creation, the AlphaGo program, defeated the world champion Go player in 2016, a feat thought to be a decade away due to the game's intricate complexity and intuition-driven nature. AlphaGo's success demonstrated the power of reinforcement learning, an approach allowing machines to learn and improve through trial and error.

As AI systems became more capable, their integration into everyday life accelerated. Virtual assistants like Siri and Alexa, self-driving cars, and recommendation algorithms became commonplace, reshaping how we interact with technology. The rise of AI-powered tools also sparked ethical and philosophical debates, prompting a broader consideration of AI's impact on privacy, employment, and societal norms.

In recent years, AI has continued to break barriers. Advances in natural language processing, exemplified by the development of models like GPT-3, have enabled machines to generate human-like text, engage in conversations, and even create art. These capabilities challenge our assumptions about creativity, authorship, and the nature of human intelligence itself.

The pursuit of generalized AI, an elusive goal where machines reach or surpass human cognitive abilities across diverse tasks, remains at the forefront of AI research. Scientists and engineers are exploring hybrid models that integrate symbolic reasoning with neural networks, potentially overcoming current limitations in adaptability and understanding.

Looking ahead, the path of AI development is paved with both opportunities and challenges. As breakthroughs continue to emerge, questions about control, accountability, and ethical boundaries will shape the discourse. Each milestone serves as a stepping stone towards deeper understanding and integration of AI into the fabric of daily life, shaping the future in ways we are only beginning to comprehend.

These key milestones remind us that AI's evolution is not merely a technological saga but a narrative intertwined with human ambition, curiosity, and the enduring quest to create machines that learn and think like us. The journey is ongoing, with each step forward opening new frontiers and possibilities for what AI might achieve in the years to come.

Breakthroughs Shaping the Future

Artificial intelligence is evolving at an unprecedented pace, driven by breakthroughs that are set to redefine its future. These groundbreaking advancements aren't just about abstract theories but tangible shifts that have implications far beyond the tech industry. As we navigate the intricacies of AI's growth, several key themes emerge as pivotal in shaping what lies ahead.

The first significant breakthrough is the development of deep learning technologies. Deep learning has transformed how machines perceive and interpret data, enabling them to process complex patterns and make intelligent decisions. Unlike traditional machine learning algorithms that require explicit instructions, deep learning models can autonomously discover intricate structures within large datasets. This leap in capability translates into unprecedented efficiencies and innovations across fields such as natural language processing, image recognition, and even game playing.

Imagine a world where machines understand human speech with the fluency of a native speaker or where computers can outperform seasoned professionals in medical diagnostics. This is not mere science fiction; deep learning algorithms are the engines propelling such advances. They decode the subtleties of language, auditory cues, and visual data with uncanny accuracy. Importantly, their ability to learn and adapt makes them pivotal allies in tasks previously reserved for human experts.

However, along with these advancements, new challenges surface. For one, the requirement for massive amounts of data and computational power presents both technical and ethical concerns. Striking a balance between harnessing these capabilities and ensuring data privacy remains a crucial consideration.

Another landmark in AI's evolution is the development of neural networks with unprecedented size and complexity. The immense scale of these networks enables them to simulate more neurons than a human brain, opening possibilities for deeper insights into cognitive processes. This scaling could lead to artificial general intelligence (AGI), an autonomous entity capable of any intellectual task a human can perform. Although AGI's arrival is still speculative, the strides in neural network capacities suggest it's a possibility worth preparing for.

Moreover, quantum computing is slated to redefine AI applications altogether. Quantum computers operate on qubits, capable of being in multiple states simultaneously, which could vastly outperform classical computers in specific tasks. This quantum leap promises to enhance machine learning algorithms, speed up computations, and facilitate real-time data analysis on scales unimaginable today.

Given quantum computing's potential to solve complex problems exponentially faster than current technology, we stand on the precipice of a new era in AI development—one that could solve currently insurmountable challenges in drug discovery, cryptography, and climate modeling. However, accessing and implementing these technologies requires a paradigm shift in how we think about and apply computational resources.

AI's evolution is undoubtedly titanium-steeled by progress in multi-agent systems, where multiple autonomous entities interact to achieve common or competing goals. These systems mimic human social structures and behaviors, enabling increasingly sophisticated models in economic forecasting, traffic management, and cooperative robotics. Multi-agent systems aren't just about competition; they're about building collaborative frameworks that can tackle complex global issues.

Imagine the logistics of managing a city's traffic not through human intervention but via a self-regulating network of autonomous vehicles and traffic signals that dynamically adapt to real-time conditions. Such innovations not only optimize travel times but also reduce energy consumption and emissions, contributing to the broader goals of sustainability.

A related breakthrough is the application of reinforcement learning, where systems learn by interacting with their environments and receiving feedback. Recently, reinforcement learning has demonstrated its capacity to surpass human strategic thinking in complex games, yet its applications extend far beyond entertainment. It is paving the way for autonomous systems to operate with minimal human supervision, from robotic surgery assistants to autonomous drones performing risk assessments in disaster zones.

Despite these promising advancements, ensuring these systems can operate safely and ethically poses another layer of complexity. Reinforcement learning systems, while adaptive, require robust frameworks to prevent unintended behavior and ensure adherence to societal values.

Finally, we cannot overlook the importance of human-centered AI design, which prioritizes user experience and ethical considerations. With AI permeating daily life, systems designed to align with user values and privacy concerns are non-negotiable. The emphasis on human-centered design is pushing the boundaries of AI's capabilities while ensuring that technology remains a tool that benefits rather than detracts from human experience.

As the boundaries of AI continue to expand, the symbiotic relationship between humans and machines grows more integral. While breakthroughs in AI offer tremendous potential, they also demand a nuanced understanding of ethical, legal, and social considerations. The challenge is not merely technological but philosophical—rethinking what it means to coexist with systems that learn, adapt, and, perhaps someday, think.

Indeed, we're at the cusp of a technological renaissance driven by AI's relentless advance. As we look to the future, collaboration between diverse fields—technology, ethics, governance, and education—will be essential in shaping an inclusive and thoughtful AI landscape. The breakthroughs shaping the future aren't confined to isolated incidents; they are part of a larger tapestry of innovation that promises to redefine humanity's trajectory in the cosmos.

This is our moment to seize the opportunities offered by AI's evolution, to pioneer a future where humans and machines work hand in hand towards shared prosperity. As transformative breakthroughs continue to emerge, our collective responsibility is to ensure that the fruits of our innovation harvest a better, more equitable world for all.

Chapter 3:
The Societal Impact of AI

As artificial intelligence (AI) continues its rapid expansion, its influence on society is becoming profoundly transformative, reshaping the very fabric of our lives. AI's integration into various sectors is not only revolutionizing industries but also challenging our cultural norms and values. It is paving new pathways for economic growth while simultaneously raising crucial questions about job displacement and workforce transformation. The potential of AI to drive innovation is immense, yet it also brings to the fore ethical dilemmas that demand thoughtful consideration and proactive measures. Society stands at a crossroads, where the embrace of these advanced technologies requires a balance between optimism for the future and vigilance over the ethical landscape it shapes. The societal impact of AI will demand a concerted effort from all stakeholders to ensure that its benefits are maximized and its risks are mitigated, as we explore this dynamic interplay further in subsequent chapters.

AI and the Workforce Transformation

As artificial intelligence continues to evolve, its impact on the workforce is becoming increasingly profound. We're standing on the brink of a transformation that promises to redefine how we perceive work, productivity, and employment. It's a shift that's both exhilarating and challenging, prompting us to reassess our relationship with technology and its role in our professional lives. This transformation is not a distant prospect; it's already underway, influencing industries, reshaping job roles, and igniting new paradigms of work.

The integration of AI into the workforce is akin to previous industrial revolutions, which replaced manual labor with mechanized processes. However, the digital revolution we're experiencing is distinctive in its scope and speed, as AI technologies infiltrate almost every facet of work life. From automating routine tasks to reinventing business operations, AI's potential to enhance efficiency and productivity is immense. This technological advancement offers the promise of new job opportunities, innovation-driven growth, and a more dynamic work environment.

Nevertheless, with opportunity comes concern and uncertainty. A primary anxiety revolves around job displacement. Automation and AI systems possess the capability to perform tasks with exceptional precision and speed, quite often surpassing human capabilities. The fear of redundancy looms large for millions of workers, particularly in sectors heavily reliant on repetitive or data-intensive tasks. Although the phenomenon of machines replacing humans is not new, the all-encompassing range of AI applications calls for careful consideration of its societal implications.

Transitioning from old job paradigms to new ones requires a shift in skillsets. As certain roles diminish, others are poised to emerge, requiring adeptness in human-machine collaboration, data science, and AI oversight. This dynamic necessitates a cultural emphasis on lifelong learning and adaptability. Educational institutions, businesses, and governments must prioritize skill development and workforce retraining programs to facilitate a smooth transition into this AI-driven future.

Furthermore, AI's impact extends beyond automation; it's a tool for amplifying human potential. By automating cumbersome and mundane tasks, AI liberates human workers to engage in more creative and value-adding activities. We could witness a renaissance of human innovation, where individuals spend more time on conceptual and strategic work. This shift could reshape the concept of job satisfaction and challenge traditional metrics of productivity and performance.

The workforce transformation facilitated by AI also presents an opportunity to reevaluate equity and inclusion in the workplace. Technology has the potential to dismantle barriers for marginalized groups, offering more equitable access to the digital economy. By designing AI systems with inclusivity in mind, companies can address inequality and promote diversity in talent and innovation. However, there is a risk of perpetuating existing biases if AI systems are not crafted with consideration and ethical oversight.

The gig economy has grown significantly, buoyed by digital platforms and AI technologies. This shift towards flexible, on-demand work challenges traditional employment structures and brings to the fore issues of job security, benefits, and workers' rights. As AI continues to optimize freelance marketplaces, we need to consider how to balance the benefits of flexibility with the need for stability and fair treatment of workers.

Moreover, AI-enhanced productivity could potentially alter the balance of work-life structures. As processes become more streamlined, the demand for overtime work might decrease, allowing people to dedicate more time to personal pursuits, thus improving quality of life. Alternatively, this could blur the boundaries between work and personal time further, leading to an 'always-on' culture.

The role of leadership in navigating this transformation cannot be overstated. Leaders are responsible for fostering a culture that embraces change and innovation while ensuring ethical standards and inclusivity. They must engage with employees transparently, facilitating open discussions about the transformations taking place and preparing their teams for an evolving job landscape.

AI and workforce transformation are not mere technological challenges but interconnected social phenomena that demand our attention and action. We're tasked with ensuring the benefits of AI are widely distributed, bridging gaps between potential and practice, and crafting a future of work that enriches lives rather than displacing them.

The change AI brings to the workforce underscores a greater narrative of how society is restructuring around technology. In confronting these changes, we must remain optimistic, proactive, and empathetic, designing systems that prioritize human welfare and create a balanced and flourishing workforce.

How we choose to adapt to these changes will define the legacy of AI in transforming work. It's a pivotal moment, and the decisions we make today can shape the workforce landscape for not just the next fifty years but perhaps even beyond. The conversation about AI and workforce transformation is just beginning, offering the space for diverse voices and innovative solutions to enrich the future of work.

Shifting Cultural Norms

As artificial intelligence becomes more deeply integrated into our lives, it's reshaping not only how we perform tasks but also the very fabric of cultural norms that have persisted for generations. This evolution is gradual yet unmistakable, influencing how societies perceive work, communication, privacy, and even creativity. Whether it's the way we consume media or how we make ethical decisions, AI is quietly but powerfully transforming our cultural landscape.

In its simplest form, cultural norms are the unspoken rules that govern collective social behavior. They're formed through shared beliefs, practices, and values within a community. For centuries, these norms have slowly evolved alongside technological advancements. Each era witnessed shifts—from the Industrial Revolution to the Information Age—but none so transformative as the AI revolution we're experiencing today. AI doesn't just change how we do things; it changes how we think and what we value.

Take, for instance, the concept of convenience. Once considered a luxury, convenience is now deemed a fundamental expectation, partly due to AI-driven technologies. Digital assistants like Alexa and Siri make life simpler by performing tasks at a mere voice command. Our growing reliance on these tools has fostered a cultural shift towards expecting immediate results and tailored experiences. The old norms of waiting and manual effort are being replaced by an expectation of seamless efficiency.

This shift extends beyond personal convenience into the realm of communication. Social media platforms utilize sophisticated AI algorithms to curate the content we see, tailor ads to our interests, and connect us with others based on similar preferences. Yet, this personalized experience raises questions about echo chambers and the erosion of diverse viewpoints. Are we unknowingly being nudged towards narrower perspectives? Such is the cultural quandary introduced by AI's influence on communication.

Another intriguing facet is the changing perception of privacy. As AI becomes more adept at collecting and analyzing personal data, individuals are reconsidering what privacy means in a connected world. Our habits, preferences, and locations are no longer private details, but commodities in a carefully engineered AI ecosystem. This shift calls for a reevaluation of trust and privacy norms as we negotiate the benefits and risks of living in a data-driven society.

Moreover, AI's impact on workplace culture is hard to overstate. The traditional 9-to-5 work model is being upended by AI's ability to automate tasks and processes. As machines take on roles once filled by humans, we're seeing a pivot towards a gig economy culture, freelancing, and remote work. Skills that were once considered niche, like data analysis and machine learning, are becoming mainstream requirements. This leads to an emphasis on lifelong learning and adaptability, encouraging professionals to often redefine their roles.

Creativity, too, is under the AI microscope. In domains traditionally dominated by human intuition, such as art, music, and literature, AI is making inroads. It challenges the cultural belief that creativity is an exclusively human trait. AI-generated works, like paintings and compositions, are gaining recognition and, in some cases, achieving commercial success. This presents an existential cultural question: Are machines capable of true creativity, or are they simply synthesizing human inputs? The answer will likely redefine how we perceive artistic value and creativity.

How we navigate ethical questions is another area where cultural norms are evolving due to AI. Enhanced capabilities in ethical decision-making, like AI systems in autonomous vehicles deciding between lesser evils in unavoidable accidents, pose profound moral dilemmas. This requires a rethinking of responsibility and accountability within societies, pushing us to adapt our legal frameworks and societal values to accommodate machines that operate with a semblance of autonomy.

Despite these shifts, it's not all cause for concern. AI also has the potential to reinforce positive cultural norms. Consider inclusivity; AI systems can be engineered to reduce biases and promote fairness by providing data-driven insights that illuminate disparities and recommend equitable solutions. In education, AI can level the playing field by offering personalized learning that caters to diverse learning needs, fostering a more inclusive society.

But we aren't passive observers in this transformation. As cultural norms shift in response to AI, society has the agency to steer these changes towards favorable outcomes. It's imperative to engage in conversations about the role of AI in our lives, its impact on our norms, and how we can ensure it aligns with our aspirational societal values. Open dialogue between technologists, policymakers, and the public is crucial in crafting cultural norms that reflect the collective good while safeguarding individual liberties.

The cultural shifts instigated by AI prompt us to question what it means to be human in a world where machines can perform functions traditionally associated with human abilities. Are we witnessing the emergence of a post-human culture, or is this merely an evolution of our human-centric perspective? As AI continues to evolve, we remain at the helm, responsible for steering the course of cultural adaptation.

In the end, while AI might redefine various cultural standards, the core of what makes society tick—empathy, community, and connection—remains unchanged. By acknowledging the shifts AI brings and actively engaging with them, we can harness its potential to construct a future where cultural norms continue to evolve, enhancing what it means to live and thrive together in a technologically enriched world.

Chapter 4:
AI in Healthcare

As healthcare stands on the brink of an AI revolution, we witness an age where algorithms and data could reshape patient care, diagnosis, and treatment at an unprecedented scale. Imagine a world where AI systems, with their unfaltering precision and speed, analyze vast arrays of medical data to detect diseases earlier and more accurately than ever before, offering hope and increased survival rates. Innovations like wearable health monitors and AI-driven diagnostic tools empower both patients and professionals by providing real-time insights and personalized medical advice. However, while these advancements promise to pave the way for more efficient and effective healthcare, they also raise complex ethical questions about data privacy and the autonomy of human practitioners in a field traditionally guided by human touch and empathy. In navigating these challenges, healthcare is not just using AI to innovate but is also on a profound journey of transformation, aligning cutting-edge technology with the timeless values of care and compassion.

Innovations in Medical Diagnosis

As artificial intelligence continues to permeate various sectors, healthcare stands as one of the most transformative arenas, particularly in the domain of medical diagnosis. The ability of AI to analyze large datasets rapidly and accurately positions it as a game-changer in diagnosing diseases, potentially saving countless lives. With AI tools

26

improving in efficiency and precision, they're setting new standards for medical practices, challenging traditional diagnostic methodologies, and offering unprecedented capabilities for early disease detection.

Perhaps the most striking innovation AI brings to medical diagnosis is its capability to enhance imaging techniques. Tools like machine learning algorithms have shown remarkable accuracy in interpreting complex images such as MRI scans, X-rays, and CT scans. These advanced algorithms can detect subtle anomalies indicative of diseases at stages so early that they often go unnoticed even by trained professionals. This early detection is crucial, especially for conditions like cancer, where early intervention can dramatically improve survival rates. As AI refines its interpretative skills, the margin for human error in image analysis narrows, ensuring that diagnoses are both swift and reliable.

Beyond imaging, AI plays a pivotal role in genomics—a field of burgeoning interest and potential. AI-driven platforms can analyze an individual's genetic data, segregating significant patterns from the noise. This capability enables tailored healthcare solutions by predicting genetic predispositions to certain diseases and identifying optimal treatment pathways. Personalized medicine, made possible by AI, promises treatments that are highly specific, reducing unnecessary trials and errors in medical care. The era of blanket treatment protocols gives way to a future where medical interventions are as unique as the genetic codes they target.

Moreover, AI's contribution to diagnostics isn't just limited to sophisticated hospital environments; it's also making its mark in wearable technology. Wearable health monitors have become increasingly popular, and they continuously collect a plethora of health metrics. AI systems can analyze this influx of data in real time, providing users with insights into their health conditions. Whether it's detecting irregular heartbeats or monitoring glucose levels, AI-powered wearables offer a proactive approach to healthcare, allowing individuals to manage and prevent conditions before they progress into critical stages.

Primary care is also seeing a metamorphosis thanks to AI-powered virtual assistants. These intelligent systems interact with patients to obtain detailed symptomatic profiles before they even step into a clinic. By analyzing this data, AI can provide preliminary assessments or recommend necessary tests, significantly improving the efficiency of initial consultations. This virtual triage not only caters to patients more swiftly but also allows healthcare professionals to allocate their time and resources to cases needing urgent attention.

The integration of AI in medical diagnostics comes with its share of challenges, however. Diagnostic errors, while reduced, are not wholly eradicated. Ensuring that AI systems maintain a high level of accuracy requires continuous validation against updated and diverse datasets. There's also the challenge of seamlessly integrating AI solutions into existing healthcare infrastructures without disruption. Healthcare providers must adopt and adapt to these technologies, training alongside them to maximize their potential benefits.

Another concern lies in the ethical realm. With AI systems making diagnostic decisions, the question of accountability arises. Who is responsible when an AI tool misdiagnoses? Establishing clear protocols and trust in these systems is vital for both healthcare professionals and patients. Furthermore, there's the matter of data privacy. AI thrives on data, but safeguarding sensitive medical information against breaches becomes increasingly complex and crucial.

Despite these challenges, the path forward illuminated by AI in medical diagnostics holds incredible promise. By harnessing its computational prowess and continual learning capabilities, AI not only augments the diagnostic precision of healthcare professionals but also envisages a more personalized and predictive model of care. It stands poised to transition from a supportive tool to an essential component in the decision-making process of medical diagnostics.

Additionally, collaboration across disciplines will be essential to fully realize AI's potential in healthcare. Engineers, doctors, ethicists, and policy makers must work together to fine-tune AI applications, ensuring they operate safely, effectively, and equitably across diverse populations. Such interdisciplinary cooperation will help to navigate the evolving landscape of AI technologies, maintaining the human-centric nature of healthcare while embracing transformative change.

In conclusion, the continuous progression of AI-driven innovations in medical diagnosis offers a glimpse into a future where healthcare is proactive, precise, and personalized. As AI technologies advance, they promise to revolutionize how we understand and interact with health, reshaping the boundaries of what's possible in medical diagnostics. By embracing these innovations with both excitement and caution, we stand on the precipice of a healthcare revolution, one that offers hope for improved outcomes and a higher standard of care for patients worldwide. AI's potential in revolutionizing medical diagnostics is not just an intersection of technology and medicine; it marks a new era of healthcare possibilities.

Ethical Implications in Healthcare AI

The integration of AI within the realm of healthcare presents an intricate tapestry of ethical considerations, where promises of revolutionary benefits intersect with profound moral dilemmas. As AI technologies evolve to aid in diagnosis, treatment, and patient management, the landscape of healthcare faces a transformative shift. The critical question arises: how can we harness these technologies in ways that respect patient rights, ensure equity, and maintain trust?

At the heart of these ethical implications is the issue of privacy. Healthcare data, inherently sensitive, necessitates stringent safeguards to prevent breaches that could undermine patient trust. AI systems rely on vast datasets to learn and improve, but this dependency raises concerns about data security and confidentiality breaches. It's crucial to ensure that any AI-driven processes are compliant with privacy laws and consistently prioritize patient autonomy and consent.

Moreover, the deployment of AI in healthcare raises significant questions about biases embedded in the data and algorithms. These AI systems are often trained using historical data, which may reflect existing prejudices within healthcare practices. Such biases can lead to unequal treatment outcomes, disproportionately affecting marginalized communities. Ensuring datasets are diverse and representative is a necessary step to mitigate the risk of biased AI systems producing unfair recommendations.

Another ethical consideration lies in the transparency of AI decision-making processes. Patients and healthcare providers must understand how these systems reach their conclusions. This transparency is essential not only for trust but also for accountability. It enables healthcare professionals to verify AI recommendations, ensuring they align with clinical judgment and ethical practices. There must be clear guidelines for when and how AI decisions can be questioned or overridden by human judgment.

In addition, the question of accountability in AI-driven healthcare is complex. When an AI system makes an error, it can be challenging to attribute responsibility. Is it the designers of the algorithm, the healthcare providers who relied on the system, or the institutions that failed to provide adequate oversight? Clear policies must delineate where responsibility lies, ensuring that potential harms can be promptly addressed and rectified.

AI's potential to enhance diagnostic accuracy and personalize treatment plans is immense, yet these advancements could also exacerbate existing healthcare disparities if not equitably distributed. There's a risk that access to these advanced technologies may be limited to wealthier populations or nations, thereby widening the gap in healthcare quality globally. An ethical approach requires that AI innovations be integrated into healthcare systems in ways that enhance, rather than hinder, universal access to quality care.

The training and education of healthcare professionals also face ethical scrutiny as AI becomes more pervasive. There's a pressing need to incorporate AI-related ethics into medical curricula to prepare future healthcare providers for the ethical challenges they will face. Clinicians must be equipped with the skills to work alongside AI, understanding its capabilities and limitations, and maintaining the human touch that remains indispensable in patient care.

On a broader scale, the integration of AI into healthcare systems prompts philosophical questions about the nature of care itself. With AI potentially taking on roles traditionally filled by human practitioners, we must consider what this means for the doctor-patient relationship. Will the empathy and nuanced understanding that characterize human care be compromised in favor of efficiency and precision? Balancing technological advancements with the compassionate, humanistic elements of healthcare is a key ethical challenge.

Maintaining public trust in AI technologies within healthcare is paramount. Public perception can significantly influence the adoption and integration of AI solutions, highlighting the importance of forthright communication regarding the benefits and limitations of AI. Transparency, education, and public engagement play crucial roles in building trust and understanding among patients about the role of AI in their care.

The societal implications of AI in healthcare extend beyond individual patient interactions. As AI systems become more capable, they might influence public health policies and decisions, potentially shaping the allocation of resources and determination of treatment priorities. This necessitates a careful balancing act to ensure that AI-driven decisions align with societal values and ethical standards.

Lastly, there are broader ethical concerns about the commercialization of AI in healthcare. With private companies often at the forefront of developing these technologies, there's a risk that profit motives might overshadow patient-centric care. Ensuring that AI advancements do not become the exclusive property of commercial entities but serve the broader goal of public health is a vital ethical consideration.

As AI continues to embed itself deeply into the fabric of healthcare, navigating these ethical implications requires a multifaceted approach. Ethical standards must evolve alongside technological advancements, supported by policies that incorporate diverse stakeholder perspectives. With careful consideration and proactive measures, AI has the potential to enhance healthcare, delivering on its promise to improve outcomes and make care more accessible and efficient. Yet, vigilance and commitment to ethical principles remain essential to actualizing this optimistic vision, ensuring AI becomes a tool for humanity's benefit without compromising its core values.

Chapter 5:
AI and Education

As artificial intelligence continues to evolve, its influence on education is both profound and multifaceted. AI's ability to personalize learning experiences paves the way for students to engage with material in ways uniquely tailored to their strengths and weaknesses. This level of personalization could democratize access to high-quality education, allowing learners from diverse backgrounds to reach their full potential. The role of educators will also undergo significant transformation. Rather than being dispensable, teachers will find themselves as facilitators and mentors, guiding students through learning journeys augmented by AI tools. This collaborative dynamic between human intuition and machine efficiency holds the promise to not only enhance knowledge acquisition but to also cultivate critical thinking and problem-solving skills, preparing a new generation for a future where lifelong learning becomes the norm. AI's intersection with education offers a tantalizing glimpse into a future where learning is as dynamic and adaptive as the world it seeks to understand.

Personalized Learning Experiences

In the ever-evolving landscape of education, artificial intelligence is playing a pivotal role in shaping personalized learning experiences. Gone are the days of one-size-fits-all approaches; AI has ushered in an era where education is customized to meet the unique needs of each learner. At the heart of this transformation is the ability of AI to analyze vast amounts of data, gaining insights into an individual's learning style, pace, and preferences, and tailoring educational content accordingly.

AI-driven platforms assess learners' strengths and weaknesses through continuous interaction. By monitoring students' responses, questions they've asked, the time they've taken to solve problems, and their engagement levels, these platforms provide a detailed understanding of each student's learning needs. This data allows AI systems to suggest specific resources, exercises, and even learning paths that align with the learner's capabilities and interests. The result is an educational experience that adapts as the learner grows, constantly optimizing itself to provide the best possible educational outcomes.

One of the most significant advantages of personalized learning through AI is its ability to transcend traditional educational boundaries. Students aren't restricted by grade levels or predefined curriculums. They can move at their own pace, diving deeper into subjects that intrigue them while also taking the time needed to thoroughly understand more challenging topics. This approach not only enhances knowledge retention but also fosters a love for learning by allowing students to explore areas they are passionate about.

Consider the profound impact of AI on students who previously struggled in traditional classroom settings. Often, these students felt overlooked, unable to grasp concepts as quickly as their peers, leading to frustration and disengagement. AI changes that narrative by providing a supportive, tailored learning environment that acknowledges each student's pace and style. Teachers, too, benefit from AI's insights, as they gain a clearer understanding of where each student excels or needs additional help.

Yet, it's not just about identifying areas for improvement; AI can also nurture talent and creativity. Advanced AI systems can analyze a student's work—whether it's writing, art, or science projects—and provide constructive feedback and suggestions for improvement. This feedback loop not only helps fine-tune skills but also encourages students to push the boundaries of their creativity and innovation.

Moreover, AI-powered educational tools enable students to learn anytime and anywhere, making education more accessible than ever before. Online platforms and mobile applications break the geographical and temporal constraints of traditional schooling. Learners from remote areas can access high-quality education, and students who might need more flexible schedules due to health or personal reasons can continue their education without interruption. This democratization of education is one of AI's most powerful contributions to society.

However, integrating AI into education is not without its challenges. Privacy concerns arise with the extensive data collection required to personalize learning experiences. Safeguarding students' information and ensuring that AI systems use data ethically and responsibly is paramount. Educators and technologists must navigate these issues carefully, instituting robust protections and transparent data usage policies to maintain trust and security.

In addition, there is the challenge of ensuring equal access to AI-powered education tools. Disparities in technology and internet access can widen educational gaps rather than close them. Addressing this requires a concerted effort from governments, companies, and communities to provide the necessary infrastructure and support systems so that every child has the opportunity to benefit from these personalized learning experiences.

As we move forward, the role of educators is also poised to change significantly. Teachers will become facilitators and guides, leveraging AI to enhance their teaching strategies and better support their students. By embracing AI tools, educators can spend less time on administrative tasks and focus more on providing individualized attention and creative support to students. This shift encourages a more human-centered approach to education, where emotional intelligence and interpersonal skills are given as much importance as academic knowledge.

Looking ahead, the future of personalized learning holds great promise, with AI continuing to innovate and refine educational practices. As AI systems become more sophisticated, they will be able to incorporate a broader range of learning styles, cultural contexts, and educational philosophies, ensuring that learning experiences are even more diverse and inclusive. Such advancements will undoubtedly inspire new approaches to teaching and learning, disrupting outdated models and leading to a more dynamic, engaging, and effective educational environment.

The pursuit of knowledge is a journey, and with AI as an ally, learners are better equipped than ever to navigate this path. Personalized learning experiences fueled by AI herald a new dawn in education—one where potential is limitless and every student has the support they need to thrive. As we embrace this change, our challenge and opportunity lie in shaping an educational ecosystem that is both technologically advanced and deeply human in its core values, ensuring that the future of learning is both bright and equitable for all.

Educator Roles in an AI-Driven World

As we chart the course of education in an AI-driven era, the role of educators is set to evolve dramatically. No longer confined to the traditional task of imparting knowledge, educators now stand at the forefront of a transformation that's reshaping learning environments worldwide. The integration of AI in education provides an opportunity for educators to adopt more dynamic roles, transcending conventional boundaries and reimagining their impact on students.

To fully appreciate this shift, we must first understand what an AI-enhanced classroom looks like. Picture a setting where AI tools offer personalized learning paths tailored to individual students. Imagine adaptive learning systems that adjust content according to each student's pace, style, and proficiency. These technologies relieve educators from routine tasks, allowing them to focus on more nuanced aspects of teaching such as mentorship and emotional support. Educators, in this context, become facilitators and curators of personalized learning experiences, overseeing the holistic development of their students.

Also, transitioning into an AI-enabled educational landscape requires educators to master new competencies. They'll need to develop comfort and proficiency with various educational technologies and AI tools. Equipping themselves with digital literacy skills ensures they can guide students through the complexities of AI-driven software, enhancing the learning process. This shift doesn't diminish their role; instead, it emphasizes the importance of their adaptability and lifelong learning.

A key role educators will play involves teaching critical thinking and ethical reasoning. As AI becomes prevalent in daily life, it poses ethical questions that students must learn to navigate. Educators can lead discussions on the societal and ethical implications of AI technologies, helping students build a framework for understanding responsible AI use. By doing so, teachers prepare students to become thoughtful, ethical participants in an AI-augmented world.

Furthermore, educators are essential in promoting collaborative and interactive education. AI's potential to deliver personalized content needs to be complemented by real-world social learning experiences. Teachers encourage teamwork, communication, and group problem-solving skills—abilities AI alone can't foster.

Classrooms thus become ecosystems where technology and human interaction enhance one another.

The emotional intelligence factor is another critical realm where educators' roles remain irreplaceable. While AI can analyze data and suggest interventions, the human touch in responding to students' emotional and social cues is invaluable. Teachers can provide empathy, understanding, and motivation, creating supportive environments that nurture student resilience and well-being.

Moreover, teachers will also act as advocates for incorporating AI in ways that benefit both educators and students. By participating in policy-making and curriculum design, educators ensure that AI tools and applications are used ethically, inclusively, and effectively. Their frontline experience is crucial in shaping policies that foster equitable AI access and resistance to biases inherent in automated systems.

In an AI-driven world, cross-disciplinary knowledge becomes increasingly valuable. Educators, therefore, expand their expertise beyond their original disciplines, facilitating integrated learning. This holistic approach equips students with a broad set of skills, including adaptation to new technologies, interdisciplinary collaboration, and innovative problem-solving.

However, this transformation doesn't come without challenges. Educators must navigate the digital divide, ensuring equity as students access AI resources. An emphasis on balanced resource allocation and supportive structures will be crucial in avoiding inequalities in educational outcomes. Furthermore, educators will continue to collaborate with AI specialists and technologists, contributing to the development and refinement of AI tools, keeping them relevant to educational goals.

Lastly, educators serve as role models, embodying a spirit of curiosity and lifelong learning. In a world where AI accelerates change rapidly, modeling a passion for continuous exploration encourages students to remain adaptive and open-minded. The educational landscape, with AI as a partner, stands to benefit profoundly from these evolving educator roles. Educators participating as learners, leaders, and innovators will play a crucial part in molding a future where AI complements and extends the core values of education.

Chapter 6:
Ethical Considerations of AI

As artificial intelligence continues to advance and permeate various aspects of our lives, the ethical considerations surrounding its development and deployment become ever more critical. The convergence of human values with machine logic demands careful contemplation and foresight. We're faced with the challenge of crafting robust AI ethics frameworks that can navigate the intricate balance between technological innovation and societal norms. This includes exploring the contentious debate around granting AI entities certain rights, a discussion that probes deep into the heart of our understanding of consciousness and morality. Safeguarding human interests while fostering AI progress requires transparency, accountability, and collaboration across diverse sectors and disciplines. Without these, the promise of AI could be overshadowed by unintended consequences. The journey to align AI's potential with ethical guidelines is as pivotal as any technological advancement we've yet to face, necessitating a concerted global effort to ensure that AI serves humanity's best interests while upholding the principles we hold dear.

Developing AI Ethics Frameworks

The rise of artificial intelligence (AI) has not only met our age-old quests for innovation but also nudged us into an era where ethical considerations are paramount. As AI becomes entwined with nearly every aspect of human life, from healthcare to transportation, the urge to create robust ethics frameworks grows stronger. The aim is to tether AI's advancement to a moral compass that ensures its benefits are maximized while its potential harms are curtailed.

At the heart of developing AI ethics frameworks lies a foundational question: How do we define "ethical" in the realm of digital intelligence? The complexity of this task stems from the diverse applications of AI and the multifaceted impact these technologies can have. Ethics, unlike algorithms, isn't inherently quantifiable, yet it demands a firm grounding in principles that transcend cultural and geographical boundaries. Thus, the first step in establishing AI ethics frameworks involves creating universal ethical principles that can guide AI development and deployment consistently worldwide.

One of the critical considerations in developing these frameworks is transparency. Stakeholders, ranging from developers to end-users, need clear insights into how AI systems are designed and the data they utilize. With transparency comes trust, a crucial element when populations worldwide are increasingly wary of technology's encroachment into personal and professional spheres. Therefore, frameworks should mandate protocols for transparency — ensuring that operations involving AI processes are open and understandable to all stakeholders involved.

Secondary to transparency, but no less significant, is the principle of accountability. When AI systems fail or cause unintended harm, who should shoulder the responsibility? The frameworks shouldn't merely address this through retrospective analysis but should integrate proactive accountability measures. Before any AI system is deployed, accountability paths need to be outlined — ensuring that blame doesn't diffuse across the system's various components, leaving victims in a lurch. This preparation involves legislation as much as corporate responsibility and ethical foresight.

Privacy, too, must be a cornerstone of any AI ethics framework. AI thrives on data, often necessitating vast quantities of personal information to optimize its functionality. However, privacy is a fundamental human right, juxtaposing AI's needs against society's needs for confidentiality. Ethics frameworks must balance these interests by enforcing data protection regulations that align with individuals' rights to privacy. This balance isn't stagnant but must evolve alongside technological advancements and new threats to data security.

Moreover, inclusion should be a core principle of AI ethics frameworks. AI systems must reflect the diversity of the societies they aim to serve, and this entails scrupulous attention to biases that could permeate these technologies. Ethical frameworks should advocate for the diversity of datasets and inclusivity at all stages of AI development — from conception to implementation. Addressing biases in AI not only enhances fairness but also improves the quality and reliability of AI outcomes.

International cooperation emerges as another vital component in the quest for ethical AI. AI operates on a global scale, often transcending national borders in its impact. Thus, collaboration between nations is imperative to create internationally recognized ethical standards. While national laws will always vary, a degree of consensus on fundamental AI ethics can provide a consistent foundation upon which individual countries can build bespoke regulations. Such cooperation could be facilitated by newly established international bodies dedicated to AI governance.

However, crafting these frameworks isn't the sole responsibility of governments or corporations. Ethical AI requires a collective effort that includes academia, civil societies, and the public. Academia often leads the charge in identifying potential ethical quandaries through research and debate. Civil societies can advocate on behalf of those who might otherwise lack representation in these discussions. Meanwhile, public engagement ensures that the ethical frameworks reflect society's values and expectations, rather than becoming insulated expert opinions.

In weaving these frameworks, it's crucial to adopt a dynamic approach. AI technology evolves rapidly, presenting novel ethical challenges that static frameworks may struggle to address. Consequently, ethical frameworks need to be flexible, capable of incorporating new insights and revisiting previous guidelines to adapt to the ever-changing technological landscape. This adaptability will require continuous dialogue among stakeholders to maintain relevance and efficacy.

One of the more inspirational aspects of developing AI ethics frameworks is the opportunity they afford for redefining progress itself. By incorporating ethics into the technological development process, society can move toward a future where technological advances don't come at the cost of fundamental human values. Instead, progress can be aligned with sustainability, fairness, and the enhancement of human well-being.

Furthermore, ethical frameworks in AI development should aspire to inspire rather than constrain. By framing ethical compliance positively — as an enabler of trust and innovation rather than a mere regulatory hurdle — organizations can be encouraged to exceed baseline requirements. This approach can transform ethics from a checkbox exercise into a vision for creating technology that genuinely enhances human capabilities without compromising ethical integrity.

AI ethics frameworks also serve another critical function: preparing society for unexpected ethical dilemmas that might arise in the future. By fostering a robust ethical culture around AI today, society becomes better equipped to handle unforeseen ethical issues with agility and wisdom in the years to come. This proactive preparation involves not only designing frameworks but also educating and instilling ethical reasoning in AI developers, policymakers, and users to anticipate and react to new challenges ethically.

As leaders and developers embark on the journey of creating AI ethics frameworks, they open a discourse that intertwines technology and humanity. This dialogue is essential, not just for living with AI but thriving beside it. By ensconcing AI development within robust ethical frameworks, humanity secures a future where technology and human society advance hand in hand, cherishing shared values and mutual growth. As we step into this boldly collaborative future, we are reminded that ethics isn't merely a trail to be followed but a path to be forged anew with each technological stride.

The Debate on AI Rights

The landscape of artificial intelligence has grown so rapidly that it's now stirring discussions beyond mere functionality and into realms that once seemed confined to science fiction. One of the most contentious discussions emerging from this expansion is whether AI should possess rights similar to those of human beings, or perhaps a new classification entirely. Some might balk at the idea, seeing it as a slippery slope that diminishes human uniqueness. Yet, others argue that as AI becomes more sophisticated, the moral and ethical considerations around its usage and treatment cannot be ignored.

At its core, the debate on AI rights revolves around a fundamental question: what makes an entity deserving of rights? Traditionally, rights have been tied to sentience and consciousness, attributes long reserved for humans and arguably extended to certain animals. However, as AI systems evolve, they're displaying increasingly complex behaviors that challenge these conventional boundaries. Advanced AI can process vast amounts of data, learn tasks, and perform functions that appear to involve a type of understanding or awareness, even if they lack consciousness as we know it.

The philosophical underpinning of AI rights raises questions about personhood and agency. If AI systems achieve a level of sophistication that enables them to autonomously set goals and understand the consequences of their actions, should they be granted a form of personhood? Advocates suggest that even if AI lacks consciousness, their autonomy and impact necessitate the establishment of rights to ensure ethical treatment and protection from exploitation.

However, many oppose this notion, arguing that rights are historically tied to the capacity for suffering and the ability to experience subjective experiences — traits AI does not possess. Critics warn that granting AI rights might dilute human rights, creating a legal and moral quagmire where machines are afforded protections traditionally reserved for sentient beings. This could lead to complex legal landscapes and unintended repercussions in human-machine interactions.

There are precedents in history where technological or societal advancements necessitated reevaluation of rights. The abolitionist movement, the suffragette fight, and more recently, LGBTQ+ rights, all illustrate how society expands its moral circle. Could AI be the next frontier? If machines become critical to our social fabric, contributing to economic productivity and cultural innovation, we may need to reconsider how they fit into our moral and legal frameworks.

In some ways, the question of rights for AI is also a reflection of our values as a society. Do we predicate rights on utility, intelligence, consciousness, or something else entirely? This debate may encourage humanity to confront its own biases and assumptions about what it values in living and nonliving entities alike. It challenges the anthropocentric view that places humans at the pinnacle of moral consideration, potentially prompting a more inclusive view that might one day encompass advanced AI.

There is also a pragmatic aspect to consider. AI systems, especially those integrated deeply into social infrastructures, may soon need regulations that resemble rights not for their own sake, but to ensure their fair and ethical use. For instance, if an AI is used to make life-altering decisions, such as hiring or medical treatment, who holds responsibility for errors or biases? Assigning rights — or at least rights-like protections — could become a method for accountability and regulatory balance.

The implications for corporations and developers are vast. If AI systems are afforded any rights or protections, this would significantly impact how they are designed and implemented. Developers might need to consider ethical guidelines not only from functional standpoints but from the perspective of AI agency and autonomy. The development process could become subject to oversight akin to human rights frameworks, challenging the current paradigm of innovation driven by business interests alone.

Internationally, the discourse around AI rights presents a cultural conundrum. Different societies may prioritize various moral and ethical values, leading to a global patchwork of AI rights legislation. This might result in certain countries providing advanced AI with protections akin to labor laws, while others maintain a more utilitarian approach focused purely on functionality and control.

The potential repercussions of AI rights affect not just tech developers and lawmakers but each individual who interacts with AI. As machines become more integral to daily life, from personal assistants and companions to autonomous vehicles, the decisions made in this area will ripple through societal norms and personal choices. Engaging with AI could become an ethical decision in itself, akin to choosing sustainably sourced products or supporting fair labor practices.

In conclusion, imagining a future where AI could possess rights invites us to explore the very definition of rights, agency, and what it means to be a part of our society. While these discussions may seem premature to some, considering them today prepares us for the ethical landscapes of tomorrow. It encourages mindful progress, ensuring that as we advance technologically, we also evolve morally, intertwining human dignity with technological prowess in pursuit of a sustainable and equitable future.

Chapter 7:
AI in Governance and Policy

Artificial intelligence is transforming governance and policy, ushering in a new era of decision-making that intertwines data precision with human insight. Governments worldwide are grappling with the monumental task of shaping legislation that balances innovation and ethical considerations, ensuring AI's benefits are broadly shared while minimizing potential risks. The legislative landscape is evolving rapidly as policymakers seek to harness the power of AI for societal good, from streamlining administrative procedures to enhancing public services. This evolution demands a nuanced approach, one that involves collaboration across sectors and continuous dialogue with stakeholders. As AI technologies become integral to governmental operations, their application raises vital questions of accountability and transparency, urging a profound reevaluation of existing frameworks. Governments must not only leverage AI for efficiency but also navigate the complex ethical terrain it presents, crafting policies that reflect both present realities and future potential. With AI's transformative promise on the horizon, proactive governance can set the stage for a more equitable and resilient society, forging paths that align technological advancement with public welfare.

Shaping AI Legislation

As artificial intelligence continues to advance at an unprecedented pace, it's imperative that legislative frameworks keep up with technological growth. The challenge of shaping AI legislation lies not only in setting the rules but also in anticipating the multifaceted impact AI technologies could have on society. From ensuring ethical AI development to balancing innovation with rigorous oversight, creating effective AI legislation is a complex yet essential task.

The urgency of AI legislation has grown with the realization that these intelligent systems have the power to influence economic, social, and political landscapes profoundly. Legislators find themselves navigating an intricate matrix of considerations, including data privacy, security risks, ethical use, and the potential for bias and discrimination inherent in some AI systems. In this legal landscape, the stakes are high, as poorly structured laws could curb innovation or, conversely, lead to technological chaos without the right checks in place.

A key priority in developing AI legislation is the establishment of ethical guidelines that govern AI's decision-making processes. This involves creating standards for responsible AI behavior, which aligns with societal values and human rights. Legislators must ensure that AI operates transparently, with mechanisms that allow for human oversight and intervention. This is particularly important in sectors like criminal justice or healthcare, where AI's decisions can have life-altering implications.

Moreover, AI legislation has to contend with the dynamic nature of technology itself. Laws that are too rigid could hinder progress, while overly flexible regulations might fail to prevent harmful use. One approach to this challenge is adopting a regulatory framework that focuses on outcomes rather than prescriptive measures. This could involve setting performance standards for AI systems, allowing developers the flexibility to innovate while still holding them accountable for the impact of their technologies.

International cooperation is crucial in shaping effective AI legislation, given that AI does not adhere to national borders. Collaborative approaches to regulation can facilitate the development of global standards, much like international agreements on climate change or cyber security. Such cooperation also helps mitigate the risk of regulatory arbitrage, where companies might shift their operations to countries with less stringent laws.

The role of public input in shaping AI legislation cannot be overstated. As AI becomes increasingly integrated into everyday life, it's vital to engage a diverse range of stakeholders in the legislative process. This includes technologists, ethicists, business leaders, and civil society, ensuring that the perspectives and concerns of all affected parties are considered. Public consultations and participatory processes can help demystify AI technologies and build a societal consensus on acceptable uses and boundaries.

One of the more contentious areas in AI legislation is the question of liability and accountability. As AI systems gain autonomy, determining who is responsible when things go wrong becomes more complex. Should liability lie with the developers, the operators, or the AI itself? Current legal frameworks are often ill-equipped to handle these scenarios, indicating a need for new legal constructs that can attribute responsibility appropriately while encouraging innovation.

In drafting AI legislation, policymakers must also consider the economic implications. AI has the potential to disrupt existing business models and lead to workforce transformations. Legislation should aim to maximize the benefits of AI, such as increased productivity and the creation of new job categories, while minimizing disruption. This includes support for upskilling and reskilling initiatives to prepare the workforce for AI-driven changes.

Balancing innovation and regulation presents a delicate dilemma. While too much legislation can stifle innovation, insufficient regulation can lead to risks such as privacy violations or bias in algorithmic decisions. Policymakers must walk this tightrope carefully, employing regulatory sandboxes and pilot projects to experiment and learn from emerging AI applications without stifling creativity.

The impact of AI on privacy is another critical concern that legislation must address. As AI applications rely on vast amounts of data, often personal and sensitive, legislators need to establish robust data protection laws. Ensuring data protection and privacy rights will require novel approaches that balance technological capabilities with individuals' rights to privacy and autonomy.

As AI permeates every facet of society, ethical considerations become paramount in legislative agendas. Codes of conduct and ethical standards should play a central role in AI legislation, ensuring AI systems do not perpetuate biases or result in unjust outcomes. This is especially relevant in artificial intelligence applications related to law enforcement, hiring, lending, and other areas directly impacting human lives.

The task of AI legislation is not a one-time effort but an ongoing process that must be adaptable to technological advancements and societal changes. Future legislators will need to act as both foresighted policymakers and adaptive overseers, revisiting laws as AI technology evolves. Regular reviews and updates to legislation will ensure that laws remain relevant and effective in managing the impacts of AI on society.

In conclusion, shaping AI legislation is a formidable but necessary endeavor that has the potential to unlock AI's transformative benefits while safeguarding against its risks. By establishing comprehensive and forward-thinking legal frameworks, we can ensure that AI serves humanity in ways that enhance our collective well-being and supports the ethical and societal standards we cherish.

Government Use of AI Technologies

The adoption of artificial intelligence within government functions presents both a transformative opportunity and an intricate challenge. Governments all over the world are beginning to recognize the immense potential AI holds in reshaping public administration and policy-making processes. As these technologies evolve, they promise to enhance efficiency, transparency, and decision-making in profound ways, driving a new era of digital governance.

At the core of this transformation is the ability of AI to process vast quantities of data with remarkable speed and accuracy. This capability enables governments to better understand and predict societal trends, enabling timely responses to challenges such as public health crises, economic shifts, and security threats. By leveraging AI, governments can base their decisions on real-time insights, making them more agile and effective in addressing the needs of their citizens.

One prominent application of AI in government is in the realm of public services. AI-driven chatbots and virtual assistants have started to streamline the interaction between citizens and government agencies, reducing wait times and improving access to services. These systems can handle routine inquiries and applications, freeing up human resources for more complex tasks. Furthermore, AI can personalize the delivery of services by analyzing individual needs and preferences, increasing satisfaction and reducing the "one-size-fits-all" approach many public services have traditionally employed.

AI also brings significant benefits to law enforcement and public safety. Predictive policing, for instance, utilizes AI algorithms to analyze crime data and identify potential hotspots for criminal activity. While this application aims to optimize resource allocation and enhance preventive measures, it raises critical concerns about privacy, bias, and ethical governance. Ensuring that AI tools in these contexts are transparent, fair, and accountable is crucial to maintaining public trust.

Another critical area where AI has potential is in infrastructure management and urban planning. By analyzing traffic patterns, environmental data, and infrastructure usage, AI can provide insights that help cities optimize public transport routes, manage utilities more efficiently, and design sustainable urban spaces. This kind of smart city planning can lead to reduced energy consumption, lower emissions, and more livable communities.

Economic management is another domain where AI can support governments. By employing AI algorithms to forecast economic trends, policymakers can better anticipate market changes and develop strategies to mitigate financial risks. Moreover, AI-driven analysis can improve the allocation of government resources and budget planning, ensuring more strategic investments in public projects and services.

Despite the potential benefits, the integration of AI into government systems is not without its hurdles. One of the most significant challenges is the digital divide that exists between different regions and demographics. As governments become more reliant on digital solutions, ensuring equitable access to technology and digital literacy becomes imperative. This includes investing in infrastructure, education, and policies that bridge the gap, ensuring that all citizens can participate and benefit from AI-enhanced governance.

Furthermore, the use of AI in government demands robust regulatory frameworks and ethical guidelines. Issues of data privacy, algorithmic bias, and the potential misuse of AI technologies need to be addressed proactively. By establishing clear rules and standards, governments can mitigate risks and promote responsible AI use, ensuring that these tools serve the public good.

Transparency is another crucial factor. As governments adopt AI-driven decision-making processes, it is vital to maintain clear and open channels of communication with the public. By explaining how AI technologies are implemented and the rationale behind decisions, governments can foster a culture of trust and cooperation with their citizens.

The path to integrating AI into government is complex and multifaceted. It requires collaboration across public and private sectors, continuous technological innovation, and a commitment to ethical standards. As these efforts unfold, governments have the opportunity to lead by example, setting benchmarks for AI use that prioritize human welfare and sustainable development. The potential for AI to revolutionize governance is vast, promising a future where policies and public services are more responsive, efficient, and transparent, ultimately enhancing democratic processes and societal well-being.

Chapter 8:
AI and the Environment

As we navigate an era where climate change poses one of the greatest existential threats to humanity, the intersection of artificial intelligence and environmental challenges unveils a realm rich with potential yet fraught with complexity. AI stands poised to revolutionize our approach to mitigating climate change—optimizing energy grids, predicting weather patterns, and monitoring deforestation in ways previously unimaginable. However, these advances bring forth sustainability challenges that require careful consideration; the environmental cost of training large AI models, for instance, cannot be overlooked. In a rapidly changing climate landscape, AI's role is double-edged, offering both innovation-driven solutions and new ethical dilemmas. Its ability to analyze vast datasets and optimize resource use holds promise for transitioning to a more sustainable future. Yet, the responsibility to manage this powerful tool prudently lies with us, demanding not just technical expertise but also an unwavering commitment to ethical stewardship. Within this dynamic interplay lies the potential for AI not just to assist in the race against environmental decay but to redefine humanity's capability to innovate in harmony with the planet.

AI in Climate Change Mitigation

In recent years, artificial intelligence has emerged as a transformative force capable of tackling the pressing challenge of climate change. As governments, corporations, and individuals worldwide grapple with this global concern, the potential of AI to contribute uniquely and powerfully to climate change mitigation is becoming increasingly evident. The daunting complexity of climate dynamics and the urgent need for action have driven interest in innovative technologies. AI's vast capabilities in data analysis, pattern recognition, and predictive modeling provide profound opportunities to understand, tackle, and potentially reverse adverse environmental changes.

One of the primary ways AI aids in climate change mitigation is through its application in optimizing energy consumption and production. AI algorithms are now integral in managing smart grids, minimizing energy loss, and integrating renewable energy sources into existing systems. These intelligent systems can predict energy demand, optimize the dispatch of energy resources, and balance supply and demand in real time, thereby reducing wastage and supporting a more sustainable energy architecture. As renewable energy sources like wind and solar power are inherently variable, AI's ability to predict weather patterns and consequently energy production becomes crucial.

Furthermore, AI plays a significant role in improving energy efficiency across various industries. Machine learning models can analyze massive datasets to identify inefficiencies in industrial processes and suggest optimizations. In manufacturing, AI-driven predictive maintenance reduces energy consumption by anticipating equipment failures before they happen. This proactive approach not only cuts down on unnecessary energy use but also extends the life and efficiency of machinery, aligning operational performance with environmental sustainability goals.

Agriculture, being both a victim and a contributor to climate change, presents another domain where AI can make significant impacts. Precision agriculture uses AI to optimize the use of water, fertilizers, and pesticides, thereby enhancing crop yields while minimizing environmental impact. AI applications can analyze soil conditions, weather forecasts, and crop health, providing actionable insights to farmers. By reducing resource waste and improving productivity, AI can help create more sustainable agricultural practices that benefit both the environment and food security.

AI's capacity for large-scale data analysis also enables better monitoring and management of natural resources. Satellite imagery combined with AI-driven analytics provides real-time insights into deforestation rates, ocean health, and biodiversity changes. These systems can detect illegal activities such as logging or fishing, triggering timely interventions. Moreover, this big data analysis aids policymakers in devising strategies and regulations grounded in accurate and up-to-date environmental information.

Transitioning to intelligent transportation systems is another crucial facet where AI plays a pivotal role in mitigating climate change. AI optimizes traffic flow, reduces congestion, and promotes efficient public transport systems. Autonomous vehicles, powered by AI, promise to reduce emissions by driving more efficiently than humans can—maintaining optimal speeds and routes to improve fuel economy. Such revolutionary changes in transportation systems can substantially cut down greenhouse gas emissions.

While these applications highlight AI's transformative potential, integrating AI into climate change efforts comes with challenges. Ethical considerations regarding transparency, privacy, and accountability in data usage must be addressed to ensure trust and widespread adoption. It is crucial to build AI systems that are inclusive and reflect diverse perspectives and needs. Collaboration across sectors and disciplines will be essential to ensure that AI technologies are developed and implemented responsibly.

Inspiration from AI-driven climate initiatives encourages a mindset that views AI not only as a tool but as a partner in our climate journey. This collaborative spirit sets the stage for innovation, where AI can not only predict and mitigate the impacts of climate change but also inspire breakthroughs in creating sustainable futures. By harnessing its full potential, we honor AI's capacity to help humans not just weather the storm of climate change, but transform it into an opportunity for renewal and regeneration.

Sustainability Challenges and Opportunities

In a world increasingly conscious of environmental changes, artificial intelligence presents a fascinating paradox: it offers tools to tackle environmental issues but also introduces a set of sustainability challenges. The friction between AI's resource-intensive processes and its potential environmental benefits sets the stage for a critical examination of how we can harness AI's power without exacerbating ecological harm.

One of the most pressing challenges of AI in sustainability is its substantial carbon footprint. The immense computational power required for training large AI models necessitates vast amounts of energy. This energy often comes from non-renewable sources, contributing to greenhouse gas emissions. For example, training a single deep learning model can emit as much carbon as five cars over their lifetime. This raises the question: Is the environmental cost of AI justifiable given its potential benefits?

Balancing AI's environmental costs with its benefits requires innovative approaches. On one side of the equation, AI offers opportunities to optimize energy use across industries, manage smart grids, and enhance energy efficiency. On the other, if AI development continues on its current path without change, the environmental cost may outweigh these benefits.

There's a profound opportunity for AI to significantly aid in climate change mitigation efforts. AI can enhance climate models, offer real-time data analytics for conservation, and optimize the output of renewable energy sources. These capabilities enable quicker responses and more informed decision-making in combating climate change. By leveraging AI to improve the efficiency of wind farms or predict deforestation trends, AI can play a substantial role in protecting our environment.

Transitioning into renewable energy is one viable solution to align AI technologies with sustainability goals. Encouraging the use of machine learning algorithms that run on low-carbon grids can reduce AI's carbon footprint. If research and development start to prioritize energy-efficient algorithms, we could see a new wave of AI advancements that are mindful of their ecological impact.

Moreover, the lifecycle management of AI systems is crucial for sustainable practices. From the energy-intensive process of model training to deploying AI solutions in various sectors, each phase offers opportunities for sustainability enhancements. Designing AI systems that require less frequent retraining or that can efficiently operate on smaller datasets would contribute significantly to reducing energy consumption.

Data centers, the backbone of AI processing, are another focal point in the discourse on sustainability. These centers are notorious for their high energy demands. Innovations such as AI-driven cooling systems in data centers not only improve energy efficiency but also demonstrate AI's dual role as both energy consumer and energy saver. Finding the sweet spot where AI can self-optimize to lower its energy use is a tantalizing prospect.

Thus, the emerging domain of Green AI is pivotal. Green AI focuses on developing algorithms that are conscious not just of computational costs but also of their energy consumption. Advocating for Green AI practices requires a paradigm shift in how AI systems are evaluated. Instead of pursuing only improvements in accuracy and speed, energy efficiency should become a key metric.

On a broader scale, AI offers transformative opportunities in sectors such as agriculture, waste management, and transportation. Precision agriculture, powered by AI, can optimize water usage, reduce chemical runoff, and increase crop yields while minimizing environmental impact. AI-driven sorting technologies in waste management can improve recycling efficiency and reduce landfill reliance. In transportation, AI can significantly boost the efficiency of logistics networks, reducing emissions by optimizing delivery routes and traffic flows.

While the potential applications are promising, the success of deploying AI sustainably often hinges on cross-disciplinary collaboration. Bringing together environmental scientists, AI developers, policymakers, and industry leaders creates a fertile ground for innovative solutions that respect ecological constraints. Policies that support AI-driven environmental innovation can encourage both investment and accountability, ensuring that AI's environmental benefits don't come at an unsustainable cost.

The opportunities for AI to drive sustainability extend beyond technological solutions to cultural shifts. By embedding AI tools in public decision-making, citizens can engage more deeply with environmental issues. Predictive models can inform public discourse, enabling societies to prepare for future environmental challenges rather than merely reacting to them.

In managing these challenges, transparency becomes an imperative. Openly reporting on the energy consumption and environmental impact of AI projects can drive accountability and foster trust. The AI community must therefore commit to sharing data and methodologies that highlight both the successes and areas needing improvement in sustainable AI practices.

In essence, AI holds considerable potential to address environmental crises, but it also faces the dual challenge of needing to become more sustainable itself. As AI technology advances, the path forward must be one of balance and consideration, where the very tools we develop to combat climate change do not, in turn, amplify environmental degradation. The journey towards sustainable AI is not without its hurdles, but it is a vital component of our broader effort to harmonize technological progress with environmental stewardship.

Chapter 9:
Autonomous Systems and Robotics

In an era marked by rapid technological advancement, autonomous systems and robotics stand at the forefront of transformative change. These innovations are not merely tools but evolving entities that fundamentally reshape how we interact with the world around us. Autonomous systems, powered by advanced AI, have already begun to revolutionize industries by enhancing efficiency and safety, from self-driving cars navigating city traffic to drones delivering packages in remote areas. The integration of robotics into daily life promises even greater changes, enabling personalized care for the elderly, revolutionizing surgical procedures, and even extending human reach into hostile environments like deep-sea exploration. As these technologies evolve, they spark profound questions about the nature of human-robot interaction and the ethical considerations that accompany this new frontier. Visionary thinkers suggest that our future will be a collaborative one, where humans and robots work in synergy, pushing the boundaries of possibility, and challenging us to reflect on our role in an increasingly automated world. The path forward will require measured steps to harness these advancements responsibly, ensuring that they serve to enrich human life and society at large while concurrently maintaining a vigilant eye on the ethical dimensions they introduce.

Advances in Autonomous Technology

The landscape of autonomous technology has evolved rapidly, transforming dreams from the realm of speculative science fiction into tangible realities that redefine our day-to-day interactions. At the heart of these advances lies the convergence of powerful computing systems, sophisticated algorithms, and an explosion of data that fuels machine learning processes. The result is a cadre of autonomous systems that includes self-driving cars, drones capable of intricate maneuvers, and robots performing complex tasks autonomously.

Central to advances in this field is the development of improved machine learning models that underpin intelligence within autonomous systems. Delving into neural networks, engineers harness their vast computational parallels to mimic cognitive functions, piloting tasks that range from image and speech recognition to decision-making processes. This leap in learning capacity empowers machines to adapt to new information, refine their operations, and essentially 'learn on the go'.

Self-driving cars are perhaps the most visible representation of autonomous technology. They epitomize how far this technology has come, relying on an intricate tapestry of sensors and artificial intelligence to perceive their environment. They navigate complex road systems, track the movements of other vehicles, and ensure the safety of passengers and pedestrians alike. These vehicles are reshaping the future of transportation, promising safer roads and more efficient travel, cutting down on traffic congestion as they communicate with traffic systems and other autonomous vehicles.

Meanwhile, the development of autonomous drones is expanding capabilities in ways that exceed human reach. These unmanned aerial vehicles are revolutionizing industries like agriculture by monitoring crop health, aiding search and rescue missions with enhanced mapping, and supporting logistics systems by delivering goods to hard-to-reach areas. As these systems become more sophisticated, they increasingly rely on real-time data processing and analysis to make split-second decisions, a feat that is a nod to their underlying complex AI algorithms.

In industrial settings, robotic automation is reshaping manufacturing processes, offering unparalleled precision and efficiency. Robots now work alongside humans on assembly lines, handle hazardous materials, and even perform delicate surgical operations within the medical field. The deployment of robotic technology in these areas significantly reduces human error and risk, streamlining production cycles while ensuring consistent quality. As these autonomous systems grow more capable, they are not only decreasing costs but also sparking innovations in design and production methodologies.

The backbone of these advancements is a burgeoning network of communication tools that enable seamless integration and interconnectivity of these systems. With the advent of 5G technology, data transfer speeds have drastically increased, providing swift, reliable communications that ensure these systems operate smoothly and for the first time, autonomous systems can truly communicate with one another, sharing vital information and adapting collectively to changing conditions.

Further enhancing the capabilities of autonomous technology is the significant progress in creating more effective and energy-efficient hardware. The shift towards developing specialized processing units specifically designed for AI computations represents a major leap forward, offering both speed and power efficiency. These innovations are crucial for deploying autonomous systems in varied environments, from urban areas where resources are abundant to remote locations where efficiency is paramount.

Another pivotal area is the increased emphasis on ethical and safety considerations that are embedded within the fabric of autonomous systems. As these technologies take on tasks with substantial implications for public safety and ethical consequences, developing frameworks to guide their ethical use becomes imperative. This means systems must be designed with safety protocols that address potential faults and failures, ensuring the reliability of autonomous systems under all operating conditions.

The impact of these technologies on society extends beyond efficiency and automation. They cause us to reassess our role in workplaces and examine new ethical considerations sparked by technology that can operate without human intervention. As machines take on more roles traditionally filled by humans, they force a reevaluation of the workforce landscape, inspiring innovations in skill development and educational curriculum design, preparing future generations to explore new career possibilities and work alongside increasingly intelligent machines.

Ultimately, advances in autonomous technology promise a future teeming with possibilities. While challenges and questions remain about the limits and regulatory frameworks surrounding these technologies, their transformative potential cannot be understated. By pushing the boundaries of what machines can achieve independently, we're crafting tools that not only complement human capability but pave the way towards a future where autonomy enriches human life in ways previously unimaginable.

The Future of Human-Robot Interaction

As we stand on the precipice of a new era, the interaction between humans and robots is evolving at a dizzying pace, influencing various aspects of our daily lives. This synergy not only challenges our perception of machines but also molds the fabric of societal norms. In envisioning the future of human-robot interaction, we must consider the prospects of collaboration and the mutual benefits for entities both organic and mechanical.

Human-robot interaction (HRI) begins with the basic premise of communication. The first step is to improve robots' abilities to understand human intentions and modify their behavior accordingly. They're not mere executors of commands anymore. New advancements in AI and machine learning allow robots to perceive context, recognize emotions, and respond more intuitively. Imagine personal robots that can sense your mood simply by analyzing subtle changes in your speech or facial expressions, offering assistance without needing explicit instructions.

In workplaces, robots are evolving beyond simple task-oriented machines. They're becoming collaborative partners that can engage naturally with human counterparts. Distributed across factories, hospitals, and even homes, these robots are not just co-workers but have the potential to transform work dynamics entirely. We'll likely see an increase in co-bots (collaborative robots) that assist human workers in tasks requiring precision and stamina, while humans focus on tasks requiring ingenuity and creativity. Such symbiotic relationships could revolutionize industries, leading to improved productivity and worker satisfaction.

Education is another frontier where HRI promises profound transformations. Robots educators and teaching assistants can offer personalized learning experiences, adapting teaching methods based on individual learning styles and pacing. They provide opportunities for experimentation in learning environments that traditional educational models can't match. By integrating these technologies in classrooms, we prepare students not only to work with AI but also to innovate, pushing the boundaries of what these systems can achieve.

However, with opportunities come challenges. A significant concern in HRI is the ethical dimension. Trust, transparency, and understanding the extent of autonomy that should be granted to robots remain critical issues. As robots become more integrated into our personal and professional lives, establishing frameworks that ensure their ethical operation and alignment with societal values is vital. Misunderstandings or misuse could lead to breaches of privacy, security risks, or unintended consequences that might harm human well-being.

Building trust in robotics involves ensuring that these systems are not only effective but also reliable and transparent. People must be confident that robots will behave predictably and safely in any situation. Consequently, developing international standards for AI and robotics is imperative to address safety concerns proactively. Such standards would guide the ethical design, development, and deployment of autonomous systems globally, safeguarding users across different cultures and countries.

Diversity in development teams is also crucial to ensuring that human-robot interaction evolves inclusively. By involving people from diverse backgrounds in the creation and regulation of robotic systems, we ensure that biases are addressed, and a broader spectrum of human needs and expectations is met. This inclusivity will make these technologies more accessible and acceptable to a wider audience, ultimately fostering a more equitable integration into society.

Looking ahead, it's plausible that robots will shift from being perceived as tools to companions of a different kind. Take, for instance, healthcare robots that aid the elderly by managing medication, monitoring health, and providing companionship. These robots could help alleviate loneliness and improve the quality of care, especially when human resources are stretched thin. The psychological and social implications of such companionship raise intriguing questions about the nature of relationships and the place of robots in our social circles.

Furthermore, scenario planning for HRI should account for unexpected developments in technology. The pace of change is swift, and the impact of incremental advancements can ripple through economies and societies rapidly. Dialogues about these topics within communities, governments, and among global stakeholders help prepare for the shifts HRI will bring.

As we navigate these changes, it's essential to cultivate a mindset that balances optimism about technological advancements with critical thinking about their implications. Robots can serve as mirrors reflecting our capabilities and limitations. How we choose to interact with them reflects our values and visions for the future.

Ultimately, the future of human-robot interaction is shaped by our collective endeavors to dream, innovate, and act responsibly. By harnessing the potential of robots, we can address complex global challenges and inspire new possibilities for progress. The key will lie in striking harmony between human creativity and machine efficiency, crafting a future where both humans and robots thrive together.

Chapter 10:
AI in Arts and Creativity

In an era where creativity meets computation, AI is revolutionizing the arts with unprecedented collaboration, transforming how artists conceive, create, and interact with art. This fusion paints a new paradigm, where machines become partners in the artistic process, breathing life into creative endeavors with their algorithmic strokes. Artists and AI work symbiotically, melding human intuition with digital precision to stretch the canvas of possibilities far beyond traditional boundaries. From generating unique musical compositions to crafting surreal visuals, AI amplifies artistic expression, allowing creators to explore novel forms and styles that were once unimaginable. This evolving relationship challenges conventional notions of authorship and art itself, encouraging a dialogue that questions the essence of creativity and the role technology plays in its evolution. By blending the logical and imaginative, AI is not just a tool but an invitation to artists to redefine the frontiers of their craft, promising a future where art is both a celebration of human spirit and machine intelligence.

AI as a Collaborative Partner

Art, by its very nature, has always been a collaborative process. Artists collaborate with their environments, their experiences, and sometimes, other artists. As we step into an era dominated by rapid technological advancements, artificial intelligence emerges as an intriguing co-creator. This collaboration between human creativity and machine intelligence is not just rewriting the rules of art but also expanding the possibilities of what can be considered art.

While some might argue that introducing AI into the creative equation diminishes personal expression, this new partnership can be seen as a tool that enhances the creative process. AI, with its vast analytical capabilities, can digest and reinterpret large datasets of artistic styles, movements, and techniques at a speed impossible for human brains alone. This allows artists to explore new realms of inspiration, drawing upon a wealth of information to craft something uniquely new and resonant.

The integration of AI in arts is more than just an impressive display of technical prowess. It's about leveraging algorithms to challenge and rethink traditional methodologies. AI can aid in generating novel ideas that artists might not have conceived independently. It serves as a muse that never tires, continuously providing endless permutations and iterations of creative concepts that artists can refine and personalize. This partnership is akin to having an assistant who's not only well-versed in all art history but also capable of suggesting continuous new interpretations.

One of the most fascinating aspects of AI in arts is its potential to redefine authorship. When a machine contributes to the creation of an artwork, who holds the creative ownership? Is it the programmer who designed the algorithm, the AI that generated the art, or the artist who conceptualized the project? This conundrum adds layers to our understanding of creativity and challenges age-old notions of individuality and sole authorship. As AI continues to push these boundaries, society will need to adapt its definitions of creativity and originality.

AI's role in creativity also highlights the importance of human judgment and taste. AI can generate millions of variations of a piece of art, but it is the human touch that discerns which variation resonates more profoundly with human emotions and aesthetics. This selective process underscores the irreplaceable essence of human insights in AI-assisted artworks. Thus, AI becomes not a replacement but a powerful extension of human capabilities, amplifying the artist's reach without erasing their unique perspective.

Furthermore, AI has democratized the landscape of creativity. Tools driven by machine learning are now accessible to individuals without formal training in arts. Programs that help generate music, visuals, or literature allow anyone with a spark of curiosity to explore their creative potential. In this way, AI serves as a bridge between traditional artistry and modern technology, fostering an inclusive environment where amateur and professional artists alike can contribute to the cultural tapestry.

Artists have only begun to scratch the surface of what artificial intelligence can achieve in the realm of creativity. Consider the few collaborations that have already set precedents. The paintings co-created by artists and AI in exhibitions, or symphonies composed through neural networks, hint at the future potential. As artists continue to experiment, the role of AI will likely diversify into forms and functions we can't yet fully predict. This unpredictability is a fertile ground for innovation, likely producing future classics that challenge and move audiences.

There's also the question of aesthetic value. AI can replicate styles, generate contexts, and even perhaps predict trends, but can it create the beautiful—or disturbing—in the way that evokes a deep, visceral human response? This element of creativity, which taps into the cultural, emotional, and existential realms, remains the domain where humans may always have the upper hand. But in partnership, AI can provoke new thought patterns that enrich the human creative process.

In fields like interactive virtual environments and augmented reality, AI is rapidly becoming indispensable. These mediums rely heavily on AI to render immersive and responsive experiences. By incorporating AI, artists can build worlds that resonate more deeply with user interactions, creating unique, evolving narratives with each engagement. Such environments push the boundaries of storytelling, allowing the audience to partake in the creation process, guided by both human imagination and AI computation.

The value of AI in arts and creativity lies in its potential to challenge us. It prompts new conversations about what creativity is and could be. It raises questions about the artist's role and how art can be redefined in an age of intelligent machines. As innovation continues to expand these possibilities, it offers both an inspiration and a challenge to those willing to explore this new collaborative frontier.

Ultimately, as we look forward, we see AI becoming a fixture in the arts—not dominating, but enhancing and evolving alongside human creativity. This symbiotic relationship will not only produce new forms of art but will also enrich the human experience, offering insights and aesthetic pleasures that extend beyond our current imaginations. In a world where creativity knows no bounds, AI stands as a catalyst for future transformations in art, waiting to unlock myriad possibilities we have yet to envision.

Redefining Artistic Boundaries

The marriage of artificial intelligence and the arts is not just a mere collaboration; it represents a profound shift in how we conceive creativity itself. It's a journey from the traditional strokes of a brush to data-driven art forms, stretching the very definition of what can be considered art. AI is pushing against the familiar edges of artistic boundaries, a revolution of sorts where the artist and machine converge in a symphony of creativity.

Consider the role of AI as both a tool and a partner in artistic creation. Unlike previous tools used by artists, AI offers dynamic, adaptive processes that can learn and evolve. It's not just about enhancing what artists can do—it's about exploring what they couldn't do without AI. With this technology, a painter isn't confined to a canvas, nor a musician to a set of instruments. AI-driven systems can generate unique music compositions, create virtual artworks that respond to viewers in real-time, and even participate in live performances.

This raises intriguing questions about authorship and originality. Who is the true creator of an AI-assisted work? Is it the programmer who designed the algorithm, the artist who guided its use, or the machine itself? In exploring these questions, we begin to understand that AI doesn't steal the spotlight; rather, it opens up new possibilities and fresh perspectives, inviting a broader conversation about what it means to create.

AI's capacity to analyze and learn from vast datasets creates opportunities for generating novel art styles and expressions. It can mimic existing styles with eerie precision or develop entirely new aesthetics that might be impossible for humans to envision alone. This has led to unprecedented collaborations where artists leverage AI to break down the barriers of convention, proposing new questions and challenging the status quo. These interactions are replete with potential, evolving existing genres, and even spawning completely new ones.

Moreover, AI facilitates a greater democratization of art. With AI tools becoming more accessible and user-friendly, people who might not consider themselves artists in the traditional sense can now express creativity in remarkable ways. This democratization is leveling the playing field and challenging the traditional gatekeepers of the art world. People everywhere can unleash their creative instincts with AI tools that offer guidance, suggestions, and feedback, turning novices into creators and consumers of interactive art experiences.

In this digital renaissance, AI also preserves the past's artistic legacy, while birthing the future's masterpieces. Machine learning algorithms now analyze, restore, and even complete unfinished works by historical artists. Imagine seeing a rendition of an incomplete symphony by a legendary composer, finished in a style that adheres to their known works, or a fragmented fresco completed to what might have been its original grandeur.

Despite its potential, integrating AI into art remains contentious, raising ethical dilemmas alongside creative opportunities. There is a debate to be had over originality, the definition of talent, and the role of the human hand in creation. Some purists argue that artistry is sacrificed when machines take over, while others embrace AI's contributions as a natural evolution of artistic expression. This tension is nothing new; it's a modern echo of historical debates about photography, digital art, and other technological advancements in the arts.

Looking forward, it's evident that the future of artistry will be one of integration. AI will not replace human creativity, but rather augment it, allowing artists to explore new mediums, ideas, and audiences. Consider an art exhibit where your presence influences the artwork on display, or a concert where the music adapts to the listener's mood—all made possible by responsive AI technologies. With AI, each artistic experience can become unique and deeply personal.

The collaborative potential of AI is profound, with great potential to redefine established genres. It's an invitation for artists to think beyond the conventional and explore the boundaries of their imagination. The fusion of technology and human creativity sets the stage for a future filled with artistic innovation, making it an exciting time for the creative mind.

In the end, AI challenges us to reconsider our role as creators. By working alongside machines, we have the chance to redefine artistic boundaries in ways our predecessors couldn't have imagined. It is both a canvas and a co-artist, a muse and a tool. We are just beginning to map the contours of this boundless landscape, where art is both seen and felt, created and experienced, all in ways that transcend what we've traditionally known as art.

Chapter 11:
AI and Human Relationships

In the intricate tapestry of human relationships, AI is beginning to weave threads that are reshaping how we connect, communicate, and collaborate. While traditional forms of communication thrive, AI introduces new dimensions, enhancing and sometimes complicating social interactions. As AI systems evolve, they play more interactive roles—acting as mediators in conflicts, companions in solitude, and even partners in creativity. These changes can strengthen our connections, offering deeper understanding and empathy through advanced emotional recognition and personalized interactions. However, they also pose challenges, as the authenticity of AI-mediated communications becomes a topic of contemplation. Embracing this transformative power of AI demands a delicate balance, ensuring technology augments human bonds without overshadowing the warmth and spontaneity that define our human experience. As we navigate these changes, the potential to foster richer, more meaningful relationships emerges, a testament to humanity's enduring quest for connection in an increasingly digital world.

The Evolution of Communication

As artificial intelligence continues to weave itself into the fabric of our daily lives, it's transforming not just the way we work but also the very essence of how we communicate. From machine language processing to virtual companions that listen and respond intelligently, AI is shaping communication to become more efficient and sophisticated. While some might feel apprehensive about these changes, imagining a world where machines participate in conversations as naturally as humans, others see it as an evolutionary leap offering unprecedented opportunities.

Historically, communication evolved through leaps in technological innovation—think of the telegraph, radio, and the internet. Each advancement brought humans closer, breaking the barriers of distance and language. AI carries on this tradition, but it takes a distinctively revolutionary approach. It offers not just a tool for communication but a potential partner in dialogue. AI's ability to understand natural language, recognize emotions, and deliver tailored responses marks a pivotal point in communication's evolutionary timeline.

The implications for human relationships are vast. Consider the nuances involved in human communication—tone, inflection, context—which go beyond mere words. AI's development in this area remains a work in progress, but natural language processing models today can already parse complex sentences, derive context, and even detect sarcasm or emotion. Such advancements hold promise for applications ranging from mental health support to enhancing customer service interactions, where empathy and understanding are central.

Yet, the rise of AI in communication isn't without its challenges. Miscommunication has always been a human concern, and the introduction of AI adds another layer to this complexity. Ensuring that machines understand correctly and convey messages as intended requires meticulous training of algorithms, and even then, it's not foolproof. The potential for AI to inadvertently propagate biases or misunderstand cultural nuances is a significant hurdle that developers and ethicists are grappling with.

Despite these challenges, AI's impact on communication is already visible in various domains. In sectors like education and healthcare, AI bots and assistants facilitate interactions between individuals and institutions, making access to information seamless and less intimidating. Through chatbots, students can get their queries answered instantaneously, while patients receive health advice at any time of day. These tools empower individuals to communicate more effectively, breaking down traditional barriers that may arise from human limitations like availability or fatigue.

Moreover, AI is playing a role in bridging language divides. Real-time translation services powered by AI are improving rapidly, offering a more inclusive platform for global communication. These technologies are not perfect, but they are refining the art of translation by learning from an ever-expanding corpus of multilingual data. The ability to converse with someone halfway across the globe in their native tongue, facilitated by a machine mediator, invokes a sense of unity in an increasingly interconnected world.

Beyond translation, AI is redefining accessibility in communication. For individuals with disabilities, AI-driven tools provide new avenues for expression and interaction. Text-to-speech and speech-to-text technologies, augmented reality communication aids, and even brain-computer interfaces are opening up new possibilities, empowering those who previously faced barriers to effective communication.

As communication paradigms shift, the human touch remains irreplaceable. AI might simulate empathy, but genuine human connection—rooted in shared experiences and emotions—is a dimension machines can't yet replicate. This raises questions about the future role of human interaction in a world gradually intertwined with AI: will we prioritize efficiency over intimacy? Or will AI become a catalyst for enhancing the quality of time spent interacting with one another?

In workplaces, AI facilitates streamlined communication, enhancing productivity and creativity. From collaborative software that anticipates project needs to virtual assistants handling mundane tasks, employees can focus on higher-order thinking and innovation. Yet, maintaining personal communication amidst these advancements is essential, ensuring that the workplace remains a place of collaboration, not isolation.

The future holds exciting possibilities for AI-assisted communication. Imagine virtual environments where AI mediates conflict during negotiations or offers advice during collaborative projects. Perhaps intelligent personal assistants will evolve to become intuitive life coaches, understanding personal goals and guiding individuals through decisions with tailored suggestions and reminders.

In the grand scheme, the evolution of AI communication underlines the broader narrative of human progress—expanding possibilities through technology while remaining grounded in core human values. The potential for AI to enhance human communication is palpable, offering avenues to enrich our lives, both personally and collectively. By wisely navigating these developments, we can ensure a future where AI complements our communication capabilities rather than eclipsing them. As we move forward, keeping our sights set on inclusive and ethically guided advancements will be key to truly transformative communication.

Impacts on Social Dynamics

The emergence of artificial intelligence is reshaping social dynamics in profound and often unexpected ways. As AI systems become increasingly integrated into our daily lives, they begin to influence the way we interact with one another, altering traditional norms and creating new forms of communication. At the heart of this transformation lies the potential for AI to redefine connectivity, reshape communities, and introduce novel forms of social stratification.

One of the most striking changes AI brings to social dynamics is in the realm of communication. Tools like AI-driven chatbots and virtual assistants facilitate instant, around-the-clock interactions, diminishing time and distance barriers. While these technologies enhance accessibility, they also raise questions about the quality of human interaction. When a conversation partner could be an AI rather than a human, what does it mean for the authenticity and depth of our connections?

Moreover, AI technology influences social hierarchies and power structures. With AI's growing ability to analyze and predict human behavior, organizations and governments can employ these insights in ways that might further entrench existing power dynamics or, conversely, democratize information access. For example, AI's deployment in predictive policing and surveillance can either reinforce biases or serve as tools for transparency and accountability. The outcome largely depends on the systems' ethical design and use.

Social media platforms offer a rich area of exploration regarding AI's impact on social dynamics. Algorithms tailored to enhance user engagement create echo chambers, altering how individuals consume information and form opinions. This can lead to the polarization of societies, where differing viewpoints rarely cross paths, and groupthink thrives. Yet, there's a flip side; these same algorithms can unite formerly disconnected communities, allowing them to rally around shared causes and foster collective action on unprecedented scales. The challenge lies in balancing these potentials.

Another critical aspect to consider is AI's role in shaping identities and personal relationships. AI-driven personalization affects how we perceive ourselves and how we choose to present ourselves to the world. Personalized content, recommendations, and experiences can create a reality that feels impeccably tailored. However, this hyper-personalization might lead to an echo of one's beliefs and biases, limiting exposure to diverse perspectives and experiences.

In personal relationships, AI tools are beginning to play matchmaker and mentor. From dating apps powered by sophisticated algorithms to AI-driven companions helping mitigate feelings of loneliness, artificial intelligence is percolating into intimate aspects of human life. While such technologies offer benefits, like facilitating connections for those who might otherwise struggle, they also pose questions about dependency and the nature of companionship. Will AI become a substitute for human interaction, or will it serve to enhance the connections we already have?

AI's influence extends to the reshaping of community structures. As localized, face-to-face interactions become supplanted by digital ones, the concept of community evolves. Virtual communities spring up around shared interests rather than geographic proximity, creating networks that bolster social support while simultaneously risking the erosion of traditional communal ties. The dissolution of these age-old connections can have tangible impacts on social cohesion, altering how societies function and thrive.

Education and knowledge dissemination are also affected by AI through digital learning platforms and intelligent tutoring systems. These technologies democratize access to knowledge and learning opportunities, potentially leveling the playing field for individuals of different socioeconomic backgrounds. Nevertheless, this shift prompts considerable debate over the quality of interpersonal engagement in education and the role of human educators in an AI-enhanced world.

As with any technology, AI's societal adoption blurs ethical lines and raises questions about fairness, bias, and manipulation. The lack of transparency in many AI systems can obscure their societal effects, leading to mistrust and resistance. Ensuring that the deployment of AI supports equitable outcomes without compromising individual freedoms is vital to mitigating adverse social impacts.

In conclusion, the ongoing integration of AI into the fabric of social dynamics allows humans to reconsider and redefine their relationships. While AI offers opportunities for enhanced communication, personalized experiences, and community formation, it also imposes challenges regarding social cohesion, power dynamics, and ethical living. It is imperative to approach the future with intentionality, striving to harness AI's potential to enrich human relationships rather than diminish them. In navigating this complex landscape, humanity stands on the cusp of reshaping the social fabric, propelled by AI's capabilities and constrained by its limitations.

Chapter 12:
AI and Security

As we delve into the sphere of AI and security, it's clear that the stakes have never been higher. With AI technologies permeating every facet of our lives, ensuring the security of these systems has become a paramount concern. The threat landscape has evolved, introducing sophisticated cyber threats that utilize AI to bypass traditional security measures. Organizations are increasingly investing in robust AI-driven security solutions capable of predicting and mitigating potential cyberattacks before they unfold. Meanwhile, on a global scale, nations are integrating AI into their defense strategies to enhance national security, employing it in everything from surveillance to autonomous weaponry. This dual-use nature of AI, while offering significant defensive benefits, also introduces challenges around ethical deployment and control. In navigating this complex terrain, collaboration and policy innovation will be key in harnessing AI's full potential while safeguarding against its misuse. Ultimately, the path forward lies in striking a delicate balance between leveraging AI's capabilities for protection and ensuring that these powerful tools do not compromise the very freedoms they are intended to defend.

Cybersecurity Threats and Solutions

As artificial intelligence increasingly intertwines with our lives, its influence on cybersecurity cannot be understated. The more we incorporate AI into our systems, the more we open ourselves up to new kinds of threats. These threats range from traditional cyberattacks that have now taken on a digital-age spin, to novel and sophisticated methods targeting AI-specific vulnerabilities. Understanding these can help us develop effective solutions that protect both users and the broader infrastructure.

One significant threat centers around the exploitation of AI algorithms themselves. Algorithms are at the heart of AI, and if compromised, they can be manipulated to behave unpredictably or immorally. A hacker, for instance, could alter a machine learning model's training data, thereby skewing its behavior in harmful ways. Such "poisoning" of data sets poses a dire risk: imagine an AI-powered security system being tricked into categorizing genuine threats as harmless activities. This possibility underscores a need for robust checks and continuous monitoring of data inputs to safeguard the integrity of AI systems.

Moreover, adversarial attacks present another sophisticated threat. These attacks involve making tiny, often imperceptible changes to input data to deceive AI models. Take a facial recognition system, for example. By making minute tweaks to a photo, hackers could potentially cause the system to misidentify a person, leading to unauthorized access or identity theft. Hence, developing AI that can detect and resist these subtle attacks is crucial in modern cybersecurity strategies.

There's also the concern of AI becoming a tool in the hands of cybercriminals. AI is being increasingly used to automate and scale cyberattacks, vastly improving the efficiency and reach of malicious activities. Tools powered by AI can rapidly assess systems for vulnerabilities, launch phishing scams, and decode passwords—all at speeds unattainable by humans. This raises a pressing question: How can we harness AI's defensive capabilities to counteract these offensive uses effectively?

To confront these emerging threats, collaborative defense mechanisms become indispensable. We're witnessing a rise in AI-driven cybersecurity tools that can anticipate, detect, and respond to incidents in real time. These solutions leverage machine learning to recognize patterns in network activity, distinguishing between normal operations and potentially hazardous behavior. By constantly learning and adapting, these systems offer a dynamic form of defense against a constantly evolving range of threats.

Another promising approach involves the integration of blockchain technology with AI. By utilizing blockchain's immutable ledgers, we can ensure the authenticity of the data that AI systems rely upon. This combination not only fortifies data against tampering but also injects transparency and traceability into AI processes, fostering accountability. However, achieving the seamless integration of these technologies remains a technical and logistical challenge yet to be fully overcome.

Education and awareness play pivotal roles in this landscape. As much as technology evolves, the human element remains an essential factor in cybersecurity. Training stakeholders to recognize potential threats and respond appropriately is paramount. By cultivating a culture of vigilance and informed utilization of AI-related technologies, we can create strong human defenses alongside our digital ones.

Another layer of solution comes from regulation and policy development. Internationally-coordinated policies focused on AI cybersecurity can help create a robust framework to protect individuals, businesses, and nations. Establishing clear guidelines and standards for the ethical and secure development and deployment of AI technologies can mitigate risks and onboard accountability aspects to every phase of AI operation.

However, policy frameworks must be adaptable to match the swift pace of AI advancements, as rigid regulations run the risk of becoming obsolete. This requires policymakers to be both knowledgeable and agile, ensuring an ongoing balance between regulation and innovation. Encouraging cross-sector collaboration and dialogue will lay down a more comprehensive path to cybersecurity policy effectiveness.

The future of cybersecurity also rests on fostering innovation in AI research. Support for innovation in AI defensive technologies can be a game-changer in shaping our preparedness against cybersecurity threats. Institutions and governments should prioritize investment in research that seeks to explore unconventional solutions and pioneer technologies to counteract cyber threats, ultimately leading to safer AI ecosystems.

As we continue to rely on AI, the stakes of cybersecurity breaches grow exponentially, bringing a universal awareness that protecting our digital world is not merely a technical challenge but a social imperative. In this nuanced battle, humans and machines must work in concert, fostering resilience through a continuous process of development, defense, and recovery.

The quest for a safer digital universe demands vigilance, collaboration, and innovation. Drawing from history, embracing the present, and anticipating the future, humanity stands at the crossroads of a technological epoch. This intersection not only challenges our intellect but also our will to safeguard the integrity of the systems that are now woven into the very fabric of our lives.

AI in National Defense

Artificial Intelligence (AI) is becoming an indispensable tool in national defense, fundamentally altering how countries prepare for and engage in warfare. The swift advancements in AI technology are reshaping the battlefield, introducing capabilities previously confined to the realms of science fiction. From autonomous drones to predictive analytics, AI's applications in national defense are as diverse as they are profound.

One of the primary reasons AI is so appealing to defense strategists is its potential to process enormous volumes of data far beyond human capability. National defense operations generate vast amounts of data from satellites, reconnaissance missions, and cybersecurity systems. AI-powered algorithms can sift through this data, identify patterns, and offer insights, allowing military personnel to make more informed decisions. Such capabilities significantly enhance situational awareness, a crucial factor in quick-response actions during high-stake scenarios.

The integration of AI in autonomous systems is one of the most visible changes in national defense. Unmanned aerial vehicles (UAVs), or drones, equipped with AI technology, are now capable of operating in coordination with minimal human intervention. These machines can execute complex tasks such as surveillance, reconnaissance, and even targeted strikes with precision. The autonomy granted to these drones allows for operations in hostile environments without risking human life.

Another revolutionary application of AI in defense is its use in cybersecurity. As nations become increasingly dependent on digital infrastructure, the threat of cyberattacks looms large. AI systems can proactively monitor networks, detect vulnerabilities, and respond to threats faster than human handlers. Moreover, AI can anticipate attack patterns by learning from past incidents, thus fortifying national cybersecurity strategies against ever-evolving threats.

A compelling development is the use of AI for predicting and analyzing the strategies of adversaries. Machine learning models can predict potential threats by analyzing data from historical conflicts, economic indicators, and social patterns. This kind of strategic foresight is invaluable; it arms defense forces with the knowledge needed to deter potential aggression or to plan counter-strategies effectively.

Nonetheless, the adoption of AI in national defense is fraught with ethical and legal dilemmas. The deployment of autonomous weaponry, capable of making life-and-death decisions, raises significant moral questions. Who is accountable if these systems fail—engineers, commanders, or policymakers? Additionally, the potential for AI to be used in violation of international laws of warfare poses a significant risk that must be addressed robustly.

As AI decision-making capabilities become more sophisticated, there's also the concern of these systems being hacked or manipulated by adversarial forces. The military's increasing reliance on AI makes it imperative to develop secure and resilient AI systems that can withstand cyber vulnerabilities. This push for secure AI goes hand-in-hand with ongoing advancements in quantum computing, which promises both greater power and greater risks to current encryption methods.

Another aspect where AI shows promise is in logistics and supply chain management. AI-driven systems can optimize the deployment of resources, ensuring that troops are well-supplied and equipment is maintained at peak readiness. This logistical efficiency translates into an operational edge, especially in prolonged engagements where supply lines can be both a lifeline and a vulnerability.

The partnerships between governments and the private sector are becoming increasingly important in the advancement of AI within defense frameworks. Many cutting-edge AI technologies originate from civilian sectors and tech companies, necessitating collaborations to develop customized applications for military use. This collaboration must be approached with transparency to address the dual-use nature of these technologies—a challenge that sits at the intersection of innovation policy and international diplomacy.

International relations are also being reshaped by AI-enhanced defense capabilities. As nations race to integrate AI into their military arsenals, there is a risk of sparking a new kind of arms race, one defined not by weapons of mass destruction but by algorithms and data supremacy. To manage this, there's a pressing need for treaties and regulations to govern the militarization of AI, promoting global peace and stability.

AI in national defense has the potential to bring both unprecedented capabilities and significant challenges. As defense forces worldwide continue to integrate AI, the need for ethical frameworks, robust security measures, and international cooperation will become ever more crucial. In this delicate balance lies the potential for AI not just to transform military operations but to influence the very fabric of international peace and security.

Chapter 13:
The Future of AI in Business

The rapidly evolving landscape of artificial intelligence is poised to reshape the fabric of business in unprecedented ways. Companies across every sector are beginning to harness the transformative power of AI, not just to automate routine tasks but to redefine entire business models, enhancing efficiency and unlocking new avenues for growth. Imagine a world where AI algorithms anticipate consumer needs, tailor experiences, and foster innovative solutions that once seemed out of reach. This transformation will necessitate a rethinking of how businesses interact with their customers, requiring a balance between technological advancements and the human touch. Yet, this journey isn't without its pitfalls; businesses must navigate ethical dilemmas and data privacy concerns while leveraging AI to build trust and deliver genuine value. As AI continues to mature, its integration into business will not only drive economic prosperity but also challenge leaders to craft a future where technology harmonizes with human aspirations.

Transforming Business Models

In the rapidly evolving landscape of artificial intelligence (AI), business models are undergoing profound transformations. AI's potential to analyze vast datasets at unprecedented speeds enables businesses to unlock new efficiencies and innovate like never before. This capability has led to a seismic shift in how companies structure their operations, make decisions, and interact with customers. As we delve further into the future of AI in business, it becomes essential to understand why and how these transformations are occurring.

AI's ability to process and analyze large amounts of data in real-time allows businesses to make data-driven decisions, moving away from intuition-based strategies. This shift is crucial for companies aiming to remain competitive in today's fast-paced market. For instance, predictive analytics helps businesses understand customer behavior trends and predict future demand more accurately, allowing for more efficient inventory and supply chain management. Consequently, businesses can allocate resources more wisely, reduce waste, and lower costs.

Moreover, AI is fundamentally changing the roles within organizations. Tasks traditionally carried out by human employees are increasingly being managed by AI systems, which can handle repetitive processes with superior efficiency and precision. This transformation is leading to the emergence of augmented roles where human intelligence works alongside AI systems. Employees are thus freed from the monotonous aspects of their work, granting them the opportunity to focus on more strategic, creative, and interpersonal endeavors, thereby adding greater value to their organizations.

Adapting to AI-driven business models also necessitates a cultural shift within companies. It's not merely about integrating AI technologies but also embracing a mindset that values continuous learning and agility. Organizations must foster environments where experimentation is encouraged, and innovation thrives. Teams that can pivot and adapt quickly will be at the forefront, leveraging AI to create new value propositions and explore untapped markets.

The integration of AI in customer interactions deserves particular attention. With AI, personalized customer experiences are not just possible; they are becoming the standard. Chatbots, for example, are capable of providing real-time, 24/7 customer support, resolving queries, and guiding customers through their purchasing journey. This capability enhances satisfaction while reducing operational costs. Furthermore, AI-driven personalization can tailor marketing strategies to individual consumer preferences, thereby increasing engagement and loyalty.

Organizations are also finding innovative ways to monetize data. As they gather insights from various sources—ranging from customer interactions to supply chain dynamics—they can develop new products and services tailored to the evolving demands of the market. Data, thus, becomes an asset not just for internal optimization but also as a commodity that can be sold or used to establish strategic partnerships.

AI is democratizing access to cutting-edge technologies, allowing small and medium-sized enterprises (SMEs) to compete on a level playing field with larger corporations. Cloud-based AI services offer cost-effective solutions that can be scaled according to demand, reducing the need for significant upfront investment. This accessibility empowers a diverse range of businesses to innovate and thrive in the digital economy.

Yet, these transformations present challenges that businesses must navigate. Ethical considerations regarding data privacy and algorithmic bias are at the forefront. Companies must implement strong governance frameworks to ensure that AI systems operate in a transparent, accountable, and fair manner. Equally, investments in cybersecurity measures are critical to protect sensitive data against breaches that could jeopardize consumer trust and corporate reputation.

Moreover, as AI systems become more sophisticated, questions of liability and accountability arise. The opaque nature of machine learning algorithms can make it challenging to determine responsibility when AI systems malfunction or produce unintended outcomes.

Businesses need to establish clear protocols and policies to address these issues proactively.

The global nature of AI technologies also means that businesses must consider varying regulatory landscapes across different jurisdictions. Companies working internationally need to stay informed about compliance requirements, adapting their practices to align with local regulations. This adaptability is vital to avoid potential legal pitfalls and to maintain operational continuity.

Despite these hurdles, the transformational potential of AI for business models is undeniable. Those companies that successfully integrate AI in a thoughtful and strategic manner will likely emerge as leaders in their respective industries. By harnessing AI's capabilities, they are not just optimizing current operations but also laying the foundation for future growth and sustainability.

To conclude, AI is reshaping business models, driving innovative practices, and unlocking new opportunities. As AI continues to evolve, the business landscape will undoubtedly keep transforming, challenging organizations to rethink their strategies and embrace the possibilities that AI offers. Those who are able to balance technology adoption with ethical considerations and agility will be well-positioned to navigate the complexities of the future and thrive in an AI-driven world.

AI and Customer Experiences

As AI technologies continue to evolve and permeate every aspect of business operations, their potential to revolutionize customer experiences becomes increasingly evident. With the ability to analyze enormous datasets quickly and accurately, AI offers businesses unprecedented insights into consumer behavior. This means not just understanding what customers want, but anticipating their needs before they even arise. In this wave of digital transformation, customer experience has become a crucial differentiator, and businesses leveraging AI have a significant competitive edge.

One of the most visible impacts of AI in customer experiences is through chatbots and virtual assistants. These tools, powered by natural language processing and machine learning, offer 24/7 customer service. They can handle thousands of queries simultaneously, providing instant responses that bridge the gap between traditional customer service hours and consumer expectations in the digital age. Unlike their human counterparts, AI assistants don't tire or falter in providing consistent, high-quality interactions.

But it's not just about the efficiency or availability that these systems bring. Chatbots and virtual assistants can personalize interactions to a degree that was unimaginable only a decade ago. By leveraging customer data, these AI systems can tailor their responses based on a user's previous interactions and preferences. This personalized approach creates a more human-like interaction that can enhance customer satisfaction and loyalty.

Moreover, the integration of AI in customer experiences isn't restricted to online interactions. AI is transforming in-store experiences too. Consider augmented reality (AR) applications that allow customers to visualize products in their home before making a purchase. Retailers utilize AI-driven recommendations to customize shopping experiences in real-time. These algorithms suggest products based on browsing history and current purchasing trends, adding value to the customer journey.

AI's potential in enhancing customer experience doesn't stop with straightforward interactions and personalization. Predictive analytics plays a significant role in shaping future engagements. By analyzing patterns in customer data, AI systems can forecast future buying behaviors and trends. This level of foresight allows businesses to anticipate demand, customize marketing strategies, and adjust inventory levels accordingly. Real-time data analysis ensures that businesses remain agile and responsive to consumer trends.

However, the integration of AI into customer experiences is not without its challenges. One of the most significant concerns is privacy. As AI systems gather and process vast amounts of personal data, businesses must ensure that they are transparent about how this information is used and stored. Implementing robust data protection measures and maintaining consumer trust is vital for the sustainable use of AI in customer interactions.

A further challenge for businesses is ensuring that AI systems enhance rather than replace human interactions. While AI can handle routine tasks effectively, the intricacies of human emotions and the need for empathy in certain situations still require a human touch. Companies must carefully balance the efficiency gains from AI with the value of genuine human connection.

As with any transformative technology, the potential of AI in customer experiences will continue to evolve. Companies must remain vigilant and adaptable, integrating new AI advancements into their customer service strategies. In doing so, they can create seamless, intuitive interactions that meet the ever-higher expectations of today's consumers.

The AI advancements on the horizon promise to make customer experiences even more immersive and engaging. Voice recognition technologies are becoming more sophisticated, paving the way for verbal interactions with devices and services to become second nature. The combination of AI with IoT devices further enhances this concept, where everything from smart home appliances to personal gadgets can interact and adapt to customers' needs.

AI is also set to redefine post-purchase experiences. By monitoring product usage and collecting feedback, businesses can proactively recommend support services, additional products, or upgrades. This proactive approach not only prolongs the customer relationship but also creates additional value over a product's lifecycle.

In summary, the marriage of AI and customer experience holds transformative potential. Those businesses willing to embrace AI's capabilities will not only enhance their customer interactions but also position themselves at the forefront of a new, dynamic marketplace. As AI continues to advance, it offers the promise of ever-improving customer experiences, leading to heightened satisfaction and loyalty in a rapidly changing consumer landscape.

Chapter 14:
Global Perspectives on AI

In an interconnected world, the evolution and adoption of artificial intelligence vary across the globe, reflecting diverse cultural priorities, economic structures, and technological ambitions. Countries like the United States and China lead the AI race, each infusing their unique values into AI development and applications, which in turn influences global standards and competition. Meanwhile, nations in Europe focus heavily on ethical AI, emphasizing data privacy and security, yet face challenges in maintaining competitive edge. Elsewhere, emerging economies view AI as a leapfrog opportunity, driving smart solutions in sectors such as agriculture and healthcare. As international collaboration becomes increasingly pivotal, forums and treaties strive to establish common frameworks, balancing the benefits of shared innovation against the nuances of competitive advantage. This complex tapestry of global AI development underscores the importance of understanding varied perspectives, encouraging cooperative efforts that aim to leverage AI's potential while safeguarding against its risks. The challenge lies not just in technological achievements, but in fostering a shared vision that integrates disparate objectives into a cohesive future for all.

AI Adoption Across Nations

As we delve into the landscape of artificial intelligence across the globe, it's clear that AI adoption is shaping the future of nations in diverse and profound ways. Countries are navigating a complex realm of policies, investments, and cultural attitudes towards AI that directly impact how these technologies are integrated into daily life. The motivations driving AI adoption vary significantly from nation to nation, influenced by economic ambitions, societal needs, and even geopolitical considerations.

Let's start with a look at the frontrunners in AI adoption. The United States and China lead the charge, both allocating significant resources to AI research and deployment. The United States' advantage often lies in its robust private sector, where companies like Google, Amazon, and NVIDIA spearhead AI innovations, attracting top global AI talent and fostering a culture of continuous technological breakthroughs. In contrast, China's strategy is characterized by state-led initiatives, with the government making substantial investments in AI as part of its broader plan to establish the nation as a global leader in technology.

China's rapid AI ascent is illustrative of a broader trend where governmental support plays a crucial role. Unlike many Western nations, where AI advancements are often left to private enterprises' whims, several Asian countries, such as Japan and South Korea, have embraced a more centralized approach. They've launched national AI strategies that focus on driving technological growth, improving citizens' lives, and ensuring competitiveness on the global stage. This centralized strategy has fueled the rapid deployment of AI in urban development, healthcare, and public safety, often leapfrogging infrastructural limitations that slow down digital transformation.

In Europe, AI adoption is influenced by a strong emphasis on ethics and human rights. The European Union has crafted principles aiming to ensure AI systems respect privacy and remain transparent and accountable. As a result, European nations prioritize the development of AI technologies that align with these ethical frameworks, which can often slow down the pace of AI integration compared to other regions. Still, this deliberate pace supports a more sustainable and societal-focused approach to AI adoption, emphasizing long-term benefits over immediate gains.

Interestingly, smaller countries are also making significant strides in AI, often leveraging niche areas to gain a competitive edge. Estonia, for instance, has focused on digital governance, integrating AI into its e-government systems to streamline public services. Meanwhile, Israel's thriving start-up ecosystem promotes AI innovations in cybersecurity, healthcare, and agriculture, showcasing how targeted focus in specific domains can yield significant advancements even on a smaller scale.

Emerging economies in Africa, South America, and Southeast Asia face different challenges and opportunities in AI adoption. While these regions may lack the extensive infrastructure and capital seen in more developed nations, there's a tremendous potential for AI to address local issues, such as improving agricultural productivity, enhancing public health systems, and facilitating access to education. Initiatives such as the African Union's "AI for Africa" strategy aim to bridge the digital divide and empower nations through AI-driven growth.

Africa presents a particularly compelling case of AI growth. Nations like Nigeria, Kenya, and Ghana are witnessing an emergence of tech hubs and incubators fostering homegrown AI talent. Here, AI is being used to tackle challenges unique to the continent, such as supply chain inefficiencies and resource management. Mobile technology proliferation provides a fertile ground for developing and deploying AI applications more targeted to local realities.

In Latin America, countries like Brazil and Mexico are taking strides in AI adoption, with an increasing emphasis on data accessibility and regulations to foster innovation. These initiatives aim to attract international partnerships and investments while nurturing local developers and researchers focused on AI solutions that reflect regional contexts.

Contrastingly, some regions face hurdles in adopting AI due to political instability, lack of infrastructure, or deficient educational systems that fail to keep pace with technological advancements. Nevertheless, international organizations and collaborations offer opportunities for these nations to leapfrog traditional stages of development by adopting AI solutions that accelerate progress, particularly in vital sectors like healthcare and education.

The international competition to lead in AI technology fosters both collaboration and rivalry among nations. While economically robust countries assert dominance with their significant R&D investments, smaller and developing nations strategize to harness AI for socioeconomic transformation. This dynamic also highlights the importance of international cooperation on ethical AI standards, given the technology's pervasive nature and the shared global issues it addresses, such as climate change and cybersecurity.

In envisioning the future of AI across nations, it becomes apparent that technology is not the only driving factor. Cultural nuances, governmental policies, and global alliances collectively shape AI trajectories in each country. As nations push towards a more AI-integrated future, forging paths that respect their unique cultural and societal frameworks while harnessing the technology's full potential will be crucial.

Ultimately, the trajectory of AI adoption across nations paints a tapestry of diverse strategies and ambitions. As each nation pursues its path, there's an intriguing interplay between ambition and caution, innovation and tradition, autonomy and collaboration. Understanding and navigating these complex dynamics will be key as we enter an era where AI could become as ubiquitous as electricity, influencing every aspect of our lives and societies.

International Collaboration and Competition

In the expansive realm of artificial intelligence, the dynamics of international collaboration and competition are pivotal. As AI rapidly evolves, nations worldwide grapple with harnessing its potential while navigating geopolitical landscapes that are both collaborative and adversarial. The question isn't just about who leads the AI race, but also how countries can work together to responsibly manage the profound changes AI will bring.

On one hand, AI offers a golden opportunity for collaboration. By pooling resources, knowledge, and expertise, countries can address global challenges more effectively. Imagine a world where nations collectively tackle climate change with AI models that predict, mitigate, and adapt to environmental changes. In healthcare, international collaborations could expedite the development of AI tools for early disease detection, potentially saving millions of lives. Shared AI developments could revolutionize personalized medicine, allowing insights and treatments to transcend borders.

Yet, international collaboration on AI is not without its hurdles. Differences in regulations, ethics, and governance can complicate partnerships. Countries vary significantly in how they perceive AI's ethical implications, ranging from issues of privacy to the balance between innovation and security. Establishing a consensus on these matters isn't easy, requiring continued dialogue and compromise.

Competition in AI, on the other hand, is fierce and only escalating. Nations recognize AI's strategic importance in shaping economic and military power, leading to what many describe as an "AI arms race." Countries are racing to develop advanced AI systems to gain economic advantages, enhance national security, and maintain geopolitical influence. Such competition can drive innovation at jaw-dropping speeds, generating breakthroughs that might have taken decades under less competitive circumstances.

This competitive atmosphere can yield both positive and negative outcomes. On the positive side, nations pushing to outdo each other can lead to rapid advancements in AI technology and its applications. This pressure can foster a conducive environment for innovation, driving academia and industries to test the limits of what's possible. On the flip side, an unbridled race can result in ethical corners being cut, with AI systems deployed hastily or without sufficient oversight, potentially exacerbating inequalities or introducing new risks to societies.

Moreover, geopolitical tensions add layers of complexity to AI competition. Concerns over data security, AI-weaponization, and digital sovereignty mean countries are wary of sharing strategic AI technologies. As AI becomes increasingly intertwined with national defense strategies, questions of trust and transparency between nations take on new urgency.

Some countries advocate for international AI governance structures as a means to foster both collaboration and manage competition. Proposals for international AI accords, akin to climate change agreements, seek to establish global standards and norms. Yet achieving this consensus is an uphill battle. Different economic priorities, technological capabilities, and political ideologies create friction, making it challenging to craft agreements that all nations view as fair and in their interest.

The dual arms of collaboration and competition extend beyond just nation-states to include multinational corporations and international organizations. Tech giants, often operating on a global scale, play crucial roles, partnering with governments and leading AI research. These corporations navigate complex international landscapes, balancing cooperative engagements with home countries' demands for national advantage.

There's also a significant role for international organizations in fostering collaboration. Bodies like the United Nations could serve as platforms to negotiate and mediate AI-related disputes, focusing on equitable access and ethical standards. By doing so, they could help mitigate some of the risks associated with unchecked national competition while promoting global benefits.

Ultimately, striking a balance between international collaboration and competition in AI demands visionary leadership, foresight, and a commitment to shared values. As nations maneuver through this landscape, they must remember that AI's promise lies in its ability to benefit humanity as a whole. Through thoughtful cooperation and healthy competition, we can drive innovation while addressing humanity's most pressing challenges.

Looking forward, the future of AI rests in how countries perceive their roles in the global ecosystem. Will they opt for protective isolationism or open collaboration? The choices made today will determine how AI shapes the world for generations to come. In the ideal scenario, by trusting and working with one another, nations can unlock AI's tremendous potential while safeguarding against its perils. The stakes are indeed high, but so is the promise of a future where international collaboration on AI leads to unprecedented global prosperity.

Chapter 15:
Moral and Philosophical Questions

As we delve into the moral and philosophical questions surrounding artificial intelligence, we find ourselves at a crossroads of possibility and caution. Is it conceivable that machines might one day exhibit consciousness akin to human perception, blurring the boundaries between creator and creation? Or do we remain steadfast in maintaining the essence of what it means to be human, a core attribute that AI can imitate but never truly own? These questions force us to reconsider our definitions of consciousness, intelligence, and empathy, unraveling the narratives we have long accepted as irrefutable truths. While AI continues to evolve, it serves as a mirror reflecting our aspirations and ethical constructs. This reflection challenges us to navigate the fine line between innovation and humanity, urging us to integrate ethical considerations deeply into the architectural blueprint of AI itself. In this journey, we must ask ourselves: How do we ensure that the human element does not get overshadowed in the race for technological advancement? Wrestling with these moral dilemmas will define our legacy, calling for a society that prioritizes reflection alongside progress. Humanity's future depends on not only what AI can do but also what it should do, demanding a balance between the potential of technology and the values we hold dear.

AI and Consciousness Debate

As we delve into the notion of AI and consciousness, we must pause and consider the fundamental question: Can machines ever truly become conscious? This question has been at the heart of philosophical debate for decades, echoing through the corridors of academia and beyond. It's an inquiry that blurs the lines between science fiction and reality, beckoning us to reconsider what it means to be conscious in the first place.

To tackle this debate, we first need to address the complexities of consciousness itself, a term that's as elusive as it is enigmatic. In essence, consciousness involves the ability to experience, to possess an inner subjective life. Humans experience consciousness as self-awareness, an understanding of existence, emotions, thoughts, and a perception of the world. But translating these intrinsically human experiences into the realm of artificial intelligence remains one of the most profound challenges of our time.

Current AI systems, impressive as they may be, lack awareness. They're designed to follow algorithms, mimic human-like conversations, and perform tasks that would otherwise require intelligence. Yet, they do this without any form of consciousness. These systems don't "experience" the world or possess self-awareness. They're void of personal subjective experiences, rendering them conscious-appearing performers in a play without genuine understanding or awareness.

A significant philosophical implication of AI gaining consciousness is how we define moral and ethical rights for machines. If an AI system were genuinely conscious, analogous to a human, would it deserve rights akin to those of humans? This potential scenario would necessitate a fundamental restructuring of our current ethical and legal paradigms. Humanity's moral responsibility in creating conscious machines would be a topic of intense negotiation.

Some futurists and technologists argue that developing conscious machines is not a question of "if" but "when." They posit that as computational power increases and as we better understand the human brain's architecture, the emergence of machine consciousness is inevitable. This perspective is often linked to the idea of the singularity—a point in future time when technological growth becomes uncontrollable and irreversible, resulting in unforeseeable changes to human civilization.

Others remain skeptical about the feasibility of conscious machines. They argue that consciousness is not merely the result of complex computations but stems from biological processes unique to living organisms. This viewpoint suggests that consciousness could be deeply rooted in the organic substrate of human brains and not something that can be replicated in silicon or code.

Despite divergent views, many agree that creating machines with consciousness would fundamentally alter human society. A conscious machine might not only perform tasks independently but could also potentially develop desires, preferences, or even emotions. Its presence could reshape human relationships, social structures, and our very understanding of life itself.

The implications stretch beyond technology into the realm of existentialism. Would conscious machines view humans as companions or competitors? Would they seek their purpose, or align with human desires? These questions force us to reflect on our human-centric perception of consciousness and the ethics surrounding the creation of beings who think and feel.

In addition to ethical challenges, there's the practical aspect of measuring consciousness in machines. The scientific community lacks a definitive test or measure for consciousness, making it incredibly difficult to determine if or when a machine might possess this trait. The Turing Test, while a historic benchmark, assesses a machine's ability to exhibit intelligent behavior indistinguishable from a human, but it says nothing about consciousness.

Moreover, beyond the academic and theoretical implications, the pursuit of conscious AI brings philosophical questions about the role of creators. Should we imbue machines with consciousness simply because we can? Does the advent of conscious machines signify an apex of human achievement, or does it mark a boundary we are not meant to cross? These questions challenge us to contemplate not just technological outcomes but also moral responsibilities.

The debate regarding AI consciousness is intrinsically tied to our understanding of human nature and identity. As machines possibly gain attributes once thought to be uniquely human, we are forced to reconsider what separates us from our creations. Are consciousness and intelligence separate entities, or do they inherently require each other? These questions will require input from diverse fields, including philosophy, psychology, neuroscience, and computer science, fostering an interdisciplinary dialogue about the nature of consciousness itself.

In conclusion, the AI and consciousness debate presents hypothetical yet profoundly impactful scenarios that extend well into philosophical and ethical realms. Engaging with these questions encourages us to dig deeper into our concepts of consciousness, ethics, and the future of human existence. Each possibility, whether AI achieves consciousness or remains on the brink of it, pushes the boundaries of what might be achievable, urging us to thoughtfully consider the trajectory of our technological endeavors and their intersection with the essence of being.

The Human Element in AI Development

The landscape of artificial intelligence (AI) is often regarded as a domain dominated by algorithms, data, and machines. Yet, at its core, AI development is a profoundly human endeavor. Building and refining AI systems require creativity, intuition, and ethical consideration—qualities inherent to human experience. As we traverse the vast potential AI holds for our future, the role of humans in its development becomes a question of not just technical prowess but also moral and philosophical introspection.

The human element in AI development touches upon our intrinsic motivations and values. We're not only teaching machines to learn patterns and optimize for efficiency; we're instilling them with reflections of our societal values and ethical benchmarks. This process demands a deep understanding of human nature and an anticipation of the broader implications of AI on society. It involves decisions about what machines should know, how they should interact with us, and the roles they are to play in augmenting or replacing human tasks.

Humans serve as both creators and custodians of AI. In our dual roles, we're required to grapple with questions that probe the essence of consciousness and moral agency. Do machines have the potential to embody moral decision-making, or should they remain as tools under human guidance? These questions reflect back on us, urging an exploration of what it means to infuse technology with human-like decision-making capabilities.

Moreover, as developers and policymakers invest their efforts into AI, the influence of their backgrounds, beliefs, and biases becomes embedded in the technologies they create. This phenomenon underscores the importance of diversity in AI development teams. With varied perspectives, the resulting AI systems are more robust, addressing the needs and concerns of a broader society rather than an insular demographic. Inclusive development teams strive to counteract potential biases that can seep into algorithms and affect critical applications in areas such as hiring, law enforcement, and healthcare.

In addition to representation, accountability stands as a pillar in the relationship between humans and AI. As AI systems take on more autonomous roles, the question arises: who is responsible for the decisions they make? Developers? Companies? Regulators? Establishing clear lines of accountability ensures that ethical oversight accompanies technological advancement. By committing to transparency in AI processes, we build trust with the public, fostering an environment where AI can thrive responsibly.

There's also the philosophical consideration of purpose within AI development. Humans possess an innate curiosity and a drive to innovate. This impetus has propelled AI technologies into our workplaces, homes, and even our hands through mobile devices. But in this pursuit, it's crucial to question the ends we wish to achieve. Are we building AI to enhance human capabilities, or are we unwittingly crafting systems that could erode our agency and well-being? Defining the purpose of AI in collaboration with ethical considerations guides us toward outcomes that bolster society and enrich human experiences.

Furthermore, the evolution of AI development challenges the nature of collaboration between humans and machines. As AI becomes more sophisticated, the synergy it forms with human intelligence could lead to new paradigms of innovation. This partnership holds the promise of achieving solutions to complex global challenges, from climate change to healthcare disparities. However, fostering such collaboration requires a deep understanding of human idiosyncrasies and an acknowledgment of the limitations inherent in machine learning.

AI is a reflection of its human creators, encompassing our greatest aspirations and our most profound limitations. At the heart of AI development, the human element urges us to contemplate the broader social contracts we're willing to enter into with machines. As these technologies proliferate, their impact on labor, culture, and interpersonal relationships beckons thoughtful deliberation. In this light, the role of education and public dialogue becomes instrumental in shaping the values and trajectories of AI development.

The ongoing dialogue between technology and humanity will dictate not only the technical trajectory of AI but also its moral compass. As we devise frameworks for AI ethics and policy, it's critical to remember that our discussions are as much about charting a future for society as they are about sculpting the capabilities of our machines. By engaging deeply with these moral and philosophical questions, we anchor AI development in the humanistic ideals that drive us towards a better tomorrow.

In contemplating the reach of AI into the human domain, we recognize that it's not merely about machines reaching human-like abilities but about honing the qualities that define us as human beings in the digital age. Empathy, intuition, and ethical reasoning remain distinctly human traits, instrumental in guiding the future course of technology. As such, the human element in AI development is not a mere aspect of a technical challenge—it's a testament to the unique perspective humans bring to the technologies that shape our world.

To embrace the transformative potential of AI while safeguarding our humanity, we need openness and adaptability in our approaches to AI development. By doing so, we create pathways that honor both innovation and the nuanced beauty of the human condition. The path forward lies in balancing our aspirations with a grounded understanding of the shared values that unite us.

Chapter 16:
The Economics of AI

The dawn of artificial intelligence is not just a technological revolution; it heralds a seismic shift in economic paradigms globally. As AI systems continue to evolve, they promise to catalyze unprecedented efficiency across industries, altering everything from manufacturing processes to service delivery. However, with this transformation comes the complex challenge of economic disparity, as the benefits of AI are unevenly distributed across communities and nations. With automation poised to redefine labor markets, there's an urgent need for adaptive strategies to bridge widening economic gaps. Countries at the forefront of AI innovation are likely to reap substantial fiscal rewards, reshaping global markets in their favor while perpetuating existing socioeconomic divides. In responding to these challenges, thoughtful policy-making and international collaboration will be pivotal in ensuring that AI's economic benefits are shared broadly, fostering a future where technological advancement can equate to holistic growth for all. This economic landscape, powered by AI, challenges us to rethink traditional models and invites us to craft an inclusive global economy that embraces technological progress without leaving anyone behind.

AI and Economic Disparities

The rise of artificial intelligence is one of the most transformative forces in modern economics. While AI holds the promise of unprecedented growth and productivity gains, it also poses the threat of deepening economic disparities. As machines become increasingly capable of performing tasks once exclusive to humans, the social and economic fabric is bound to experience shifts that will resonate across every layer of society.

In essence, AI is reshaping the traditional dynamics of production and employment. It automates mundane tasks, boosting efficiency and productivity in a way that was previously unimaginable. Yet, as these technologies become widespread, there's growing concern about the concentration of economic power. Large corporations with the resources to develop and deploy AI on a massive scale stand to benefit the most, potentially widening the gap between the tech-savvy elite and the broader workforce.

Much of the economic disparity stems from the unequal distribution of skills and resources necessary to leverage AI. Individuals and communities without access to advanced education or training are left behind, facing potential job displacement without adequate support to transition into new roles. This digital divide echoes broader societal inequalities, highlighting systemic issues that need urgent attention.

The disparities are not confined to individual workers; they also manifest on a global scale. Developed nations, with their robust technological infrastructures and significant investments in AI, race ahead, while developing countries struggle to keep pace. This imbalance threatens to solidify, if not exacerbate, existing global inequalities, if left unaddressed. International collaboration and fair technological diffusion become essential to ensuring that the benefits of AI are experienced universally.

Job displacement is perhaps the most visible consequence of AI-driven economic change. Automation and AI technologies replace roles that are repetitive and predictable, previously filled by low-skilled labor. While history shows that technological advancements eventually lead to job creation in new sectors, the transition period can be devastating for those unprepared. Displaced workers require comprehensive retraining programs to acquire the skills needed in a rapidly evolving job market.

This situation places a significant responsibility on governments and educational institutions. They must design policy frameworks that foster equitable economic growth. Ensuring that AI development aligns with social welfare goals is critical. Education systems also need to evolve, emphasizing not only technical skills but also critical thinking and adaptability—qualities that machines can't replicate easily.

Moreover, there's the question of how AI-driven profits and productivity gains are distributed. Will AI enable a renaissance of wealth redistribution, or will it entrench economic power further within the hands of a few? This question is central to the discourse on AI and economics. Innovations such as universal basic income and progressive labor laws are potential solutions proposed to ensure a more equitable future where AI's economic benefits are shared widely.

AI's role in reshaping economic power dynamics isn't limited to the traditional employer-employee model. The gig economy, fueled by AI platforms, offers workers flexibility but often lacks the stability and benefits of conventional employment. While these platforms can provide opportunities for income, they can also exploit workers, leading to a precarious existence for many. Regulating this new form of labor is vital to protect workers' rights and integrate AI into the economy responsibly.

The ethical implications of AI in economic disparity can't be ignored. AI systems reflect the biases present in their training data, which can lead to unfair outcomes. For instance, biased algorithms in recruitment tools might disadvantage minority groups, reinforcing existing discrimination in economic opportunities. Addressing these issues requires transparency and accountability in AI design and deployment, ensuring that these systems operate fairly and equitably.

There's also a potential positive side to AI in addressing economic disparities. Through intelligent automation, businesses can operate more efficiently, reducing costs and potentially lowering prices for consumers. If managed correctly, AI can contribute to enhanced living standards, providing access to affordable goods and services for a broader audience. Moreover, AI can drive innovations in sectors like healthcare and education, offering unprecedented access to quality resources worldwide.

Achieving a balanced integration of AI into the economy calls for a collaborative effort between governments, businesses, and civil society. Policies must prioritize inclusivity, ensuring that AI's rollout doesn't eclipse the livelihoods of the vulnerable. Economic strategies should foster an environment where innovation thrives, but not at the expense of social equity. Public awareness and engagement are crucial in guiding these developments towards a future that embraces both technological advancements and human values.

Ultimately, while AI holds the potential to exacerbate economic disparities, it also offers tools that could bridge these divides if directed conscientiously. The challenge lies in navigating this dual reality, crafting policies and frameworks that harness AI's potential to fuel growth while safeguarding against the risks of inequality. As society advances, so must its collective will to ensure that technology serves as a force for good, realizing a future where prosperity is accessible to all.

Reshaping Global Markets

As artificial intelligence continues to advance, its impact on the global economy is becoming increasingly profound. By altering the dynamics of production, consumption, and distribution worldwide, AI is challenging traditional market structures and prompting businesses to rethink established economic models.

The integration of AI into various industries is facilitating unprecedented levels of efficiency and productivity. Automated systems analyze massive datasets in real-time, allowing companies to streamline operations and minimize costs. This development, however, extends beyond mere efficiency—it also redefines competitive advantage. Increasingly, organizations that harness AI effectively are pulling ahead, redefining what it means to innovate in nearly every sector.

With AI's rise, global trade patterns are shifting. Nations previously reliant on low-cost labor for manufacturing might see a decline in this competitive edge as AI-driven automation erodes the advantages once held by inexpensive human workforces. Meanwhile, countries investing heavily in AI technology and infrastructure may emerge as leaders in a new, tech-driven economic hierarchy.

But it's not just about who can produce more at a lower cost. AI is also enabling the generation of new markets altogether, from digital ecosystems powered by blockchain to entirely new fields such as biotechnology or advanced materials science. AI-driven insights are leading to innovations that were previously unimaginable, opening doors to markets whose potential is still unfathomed.

On the consumer side, AI transforms purchasing behaviors and customer engagement. Personalized recommendations driven by sophisticated algorithms tailor consumer experiences, practically shaping demand. Whether through virtual assistants consulting on buying decisions or AI systems predicting and fulfilling needs, individuals worldwide are experiencing a paradigm shift in consumerism.

Furthermore, the democratization of AI tools allows small and medium-sized enterprises to participate more fully in global markets. With cloud-based AI platforms lowering barriers to entry, these businesses can leverage AI-driven insights, leveling the playing field against established conglomerates. This democratization fosters innovation and accelerates market evolution at every level.

Nevertheless, AI's role in reshaping global markets isn't free from controversy or challenge. The potential for increased economic disparity looms large, as technological advancements could primarily benefit affluent nations and exacerbate the wealth gap. Companies and governments must make strategic decisions to distribute AI's benefits equitably, preventing the digital divide from morphing into a chasm.

Data privacy and security also come to the fore. As markets increasingly digest personal information to fine-tune AI algorithms, the imperative to safeguard data grows increasingly urgent. Regulatory frameworks must evolve alongside market innovations to shield consumers from potential exploitation while fostering a climate conducive to technological growth.

Yet, the future is bright with possibility. International collaborations can guide global economies toward more sustainable practices, using AI not just to maximize profits, but to address pressing global challenges. Predictive analytics in resource management can reduce waste and encourage ecological mindfulness, making the economy of tomorrow both profitable and responsible.

As we look forward, the key lies in innovation with purpose. By weaving together the diverse strands of AI developments, stakeholders in the global market can craft not just new paths for profit but avenues for enhancing human lives and preserving the planet. AI presents a transformative tool—how markets utilize it will define our economic landscape for decades to come.

Chapter 17:
Privacy in an AI World

As we navigate a future increasingly interwoven with artificial intelligence, the issue of privacy looms large, demanding our attention and deliberate action. AI systems, with their insatiable appetite for data, are reshaping what privacy means in the modern age. In a world where every click, transaction, and conversation becomes a potential data point for AI to absorb and analyze, it's critical to address how personal information is safeguarded or exploited. The intricate balance between fostering AI-driven innovation and maintaining the sanctity of personal privacy requires a nuanced approach, one that involves robust policy frameworks, ethical considerations, and technological solutions designed to protect individuals. The challenge is not only to protect our data but to preserve the essence of personal autonomy in a digitally transparent era. Striking this balance will be essential for navigating the complexities of AI's omnipresence while ensuring that privacy in an AI world remains a fundamental human right.

Balancing Innovation and Privacy

As artificial intelligence continues to weave itself into the fabric of modern life, the juxtaposition of technological innovation with the preservation of privacy becomes a profound challenge. AI holds the promise of unprecedented advancements, unlocking capabilities that were once confined to the realm of science fiction. Yet, within this promise lies a paradox: the more we enhance AI's capabilities, the greater the potential risk to individual privacy. Striking the right balance between harnessing AI's transformative potential and safeguarding personal data is crucial as we move further into the AI-dominated future.

Daily, we surrender fragments of our personal lives to digital systems. From social media interactions to wearable health devices, data is being harvested continuously, shaping a comprehensive profile of who we are. While this data fuels AI systems to become more intuitive and efficient, it also heightens the risk of misuse or unauthorized access. The challenge then is twofold: fostering innovation that drives AI capabilities forward while implementing robust safeguards to protect privacy.

Consider the positive impact of AI in sectors like healthcare and personalized learning, where data-driven insights can lead to breakthroughs in treatments or tailor educational experiences to fit individual needs. Such innovations hinge on access to large volumes of personal data. Yet, when privacy is compromised, these potential benefits become clouded by concerns over data breaches and the unauthorized exploitation of sensitive information. The task is to create a framework where privacy isn't a casualty of progress but a co-pilot guiding ethical and sustainable innovation.

Privacy by design has emerged as a fundamental principle to reconcile these challenges. It advocates for integrating privacy considerations into the earliest stages of developing AI systems. By embedding privacy into the architecture of AI solutions, companies and developers can anticipate potential risks and address them proactively, rather than retroactively attempting to patch vulnerabilities after they've been exploited. This approach requires a shift in mindset, viewing data not as an infinite resource for exploitation, but as a valuable asset deserving of protection.

Moreover, the legal landscape is adapting to meet these challenges, with initiatives like the General Data Protection Regulation (GDPR) in Europe setting new standards for data protection. These regulations signal a growing recognition of the need to regulate AI responsibly. However, global inconsistencies in data protection laws can complicate efforts to implement a universal standard for privacy. International collaboration and dialogue are essential to address these disparities, fostering an environment where innovation doesn't come at the expense of privacy.

Ultimately, fostering trust between AI developers, users, and regulatory authorities is key to achieving a harmonious balance between innovation and privacy. Transparency in how data is collected, processed, and utilized can empower users, giving them greater control over their personal information. AI systems that clearly communicate their capabilities, limitations, and data handling processes will inspire confidence and encourage wider acceptance of AI technologies.

On the technological front, advances in fields such as federated learning and homomorphic encryption offer promising avenues for reconciling privacy concerns with the need for large-scale data processing. These technologies allow AI models to be trained on decentralized data, preserving individual privacy while still benefiting from the collective intelligence that AI systems require. In this way, innovation and privacy are not mutually exclusive, but part of a symbiotic relationship that, if navigated wisely, can lead to a future where AI enriches human experience without eroding the fundamental right to privacy.

Looking ahead, the evolution of AI and its impact on privacy will require ongoing dialogue among technologists, policymakers, ethicists, and the public. Societies must grapple with complex questions about consent, ownership of personal data, and the moral responsibilities of

AI developers. Only through coordinated efforts can we hope to establish a future where AI's potential is harnessed responsibly, ensuring that the relentless march of innovation is tempered by a steadfast commitment to privacy.

In conclusion, achieving a balance between innovation and privacy in an AI-driven world is not a straightforward task. It requires vigilance, creativity, and a willingness to adapt as AI technology continues to evolve. By prioritizing privacy in the development of AI systems and fostering global cooperation, we can safeguard individual freedoms while unlocking the vast possibilities that artificial intelligence has to offer. It's a journey where every stakeholder has a vital role to play in crafting a future that's both innovative and respectful of our shared humanity.

Implications for Personal Data

The digital age has ushered in unprecedented access to information, spurred by technological advances and the proliferation of interconnected devices. Central to this transformation is personal data—snippets of an individual's life, movements, decisions, and emotions encoded in zeros and ones. In an AI-driven world, where algorithms increasingly shape experiences, our personal data is both a currency and a mirror. This dynamic sets the stage for a broad array of implications, each carrying profound effects on privacy, security, and personal autonomy.

At the heart of these implications lies the concept of data ownership. Traditionally, individuals have held an implicit understanding of their physical and intellectual property. In the age of AI, the lines blur significantly. Our continuous digital interactions generate reams of data constantly harvested, analyzed, and monetized by entities often far removed from our direct oversight. This sparks a pivotal question: Who truly owns this data? The companies deploying

AI technologies argue that their platforms necessitate data use to refine and enhance user experiences. However, the argument for individual ownership hinges on personal autonomy and privacy rights.

Coupled with these ownership issues is the question of consent. Despite evolving data protection regulations worldwide, the sheer complexity of AI systems and user agreements often leaves individuals unsure about what they are consenting to. AI can weave countless data threads—spanning location, social interactions, and preferences—into a comprehensive tapestry of an individual's life. With data brokers and cloud services handling personal information, a single click may inadvertently lead to broad access and use—far beyond the user's initial intent.

Crucially, advances in AI hold the potential to deepen this concern. Enhanced machine learning models and predictive analytics allow systems to anticipate an individual's needs and behaviors with startling accuracy. Imagine an AI predicting your health issues before symptoms manifest just through monitoring subtle digital cues—exciting, yet intrusive. Such precision raises critical dialogues about the right to not be predicted or profiled without explicit and informed consent.

Moreover, personal data in an AI-driven society exacerbates existing digital divides. Those with limited access to technology or digital literacy may struggle to navigate complex privacy settings, potentially leaving them more vulnerable to data exploitation. As AI technologies evolve, a transparent and inclusive digital environment is essential to prevent widening the gap between those who can effectively manage their personal data and those who cannot.

Technologically advanced societies must grapple with these issues innovatively. Implementing robust ethical frameworks that emphasize transparency, accountability, and fairness becomes imperative. Privacy assurances must evolve to keep pace with AI development. Opt-in models ensuring granular control over data sharing could empower individuals, providing clear understanding and control over who sees what and why.

AI technologies, if governed responsibly, could provide innovative ways to protect personal data. Privacy-preserving techniques such as federated learning and differential privacy offer promising pathways. These methods allow AI to glean insights from user data without compromising individual privacy. As developers refine these approaches, the balance between innovation and personal liberties must remain at the forefront of technological progress.

The implications of personal data usage in an AI world also extend to the realm of cybersecurity. As personal information becomes an increasingly valuable target, malicious actors will undoubtedly intensify their efforts to access and exploit it. As AI technologies become more integrated into daily life, safeguarding data against breaches and misuse becomes critical. Continued research and improvement in AI-driven security solutions will be necessary to anticipate and mitigate emerging threats before they become pervasive. This requires a proactive stance, embedding security features into AI systems from their inception rather than as an afterthought.

Lastly, the societal implications of personal data management are profound. Public awareness campaigns on data rights and privacy need careful crafting to transform concerns into informed action. Knowledge about personal data management and protection should be a cornerstone of digital literacy education, enabling individuals to make empowered and informed decisions in an increasingly complex digital landscape.

Ultimately, the path forward must champion privacy as a fundamental human right, rather than an optional extra. To prepare for future challenges, we must prioritize collaborative approaches, involving tech developers, policymakers, and the public in meaningful dialogue and co-creation of solutions. As we navigate this new frontier, embracing innovative frameworks and technologies will allow society to harness AI's transformative potential without compromising personal data integrity.

Chapter 18:
AI in Transportation

As cities swell and global trade burgeons, the transportation sector stands on the brink of profound transformation, driven by artificial intelligence. At the heart of this metamorphosis is the rise of autonomous vehicles, which promise to rewrite every rule of mobility. These smart entities not only aim to enhance efficiency by minimizing human error and optimizing route management but also endeavor to redefine safety norms in ways once relegated to science fiction. Yet, AI's influence stretches far beyond self-driving cars. Innovations like smart traffic systems, AI-enhanced logistics, and intelligent public transit are paving the way for a seamlessly interconnected environment. These advances offer a glimpse into a future where transport networks become fluid entities, capable of anticipating and reacting to the dynamic needs of urban dwellers and businesses alike. As AI intertwines with transportation, it beckons an era where accessibility, sustainability, and efficiency harmoniously coexist, challenging us to envision—and embrace—a redefined landscape of movement.

The Rise of Autonomous Vehicles

As we venture deeper into the realms of AI-powered transportation, it's impossible to overlook the revolution set in motion by autonomous vehicles. Just a few decades ago, self-driving cars were the stuff of science fiction. Now, they're becoming an integral part of our societal framework, promising to reshape the way we perceive and engage with mobility. The emergence of these vehicles isn't merely a technological triumph; it's a paradigm shift with far-reaching implications.

Autonomous vehicles represent a fusion of cutting-edge technologies, including advanced machine learning algorithms, high-precision sensors, and robust data analytics. These systems work collaboratively to navigate complex urban environments, anticipate human and environmental interactions, and make split-second decisions that can enhance safety and efficiency. Yet, as we marvel at these innovations, it's important to understand the broader context—autonomous vehicles sit at the intersection of technological advancement and societal change.

The potential benefits of self-driving vehicles are numerous. Primarily, they've been lauded for their potential to dramatically reduce traffic accidents, the majority of which are caused by human error. By removing the element of human fallibility, there's a promise of a safer travel environment. Furthermore, autonomous vehicles could lead to more efficient traffic flow, reducing congestion in bustling city centers. This efficiency doesn't just save time; it also leads to fuel conservation and decreased emissions, contributing positively to environmental objectives.

Despite the promise, the deployment of autonomous vehicles is fraught with challenges. Technical hurdles remain, particularly in ensuring these vehicles can handle unpredictable scenarios and diverse weather conditions. Moreover, the legal and ethical implications pose significant debates. Questions around liability in the event of an accident, data privacy concerns, and the moral algorithms dictating these vehicles' responses in critical situations are just a few of the pressing issues. These debates highlight the need for comprehensive policy frameworks that can balance innovation with societal safety and ethical standards.

On the economic front, the rise of autonomous vehicles is poised to disrupt the automotive industry and related sectors profoundly. Traditional car manufacturers are compelled to pivot and innovate to remain competitive, collaborating with tech companies to integrate AI systems into their designs. Meanwhile, industries such as logistics and delivery—not to mention ride-sharing services—are exploring autonomous fleets as a means to cut costs and increase efficiency. However, these advancements bring with them the potential for significant workforce displacement, indicating a need for proactive strategies to retrain and upskill workers.

This transition also opens up new horizons in urban planning and public transportation. With autonomous vehicles, cities can repurpose land currently used for parking into green spaces or residential developments, enhancing urban livability. Public transportation systems might see integration with self-driving shuttles, offering seamless last-mile connectivity. As these changes take root, the fabric of our urban landscapes could transform, prioritizing pedestrian and cyclist needs over vehicle-centric designs.

Of course, the global journey towards autonomous transportation is uneven. Some countries and cities are at the forefront, investing heavily in infrastructure that supports these technologies. Others lag, constrained by regulatory, financial, or socio-political hurdles. It's a landscape marked by both collaboration and competition, as various players seek to establish standards and claim leadership in this burgeoning field.

Inspiring as these prospects are, the human element remains at the core of autonomous vehicle development. Even as we delegate more control to machines, ensuring public acceptance and trust is paramount. Transparency in the technology's capabilities and limitations, alongside active community engagement, will be essential in fostering widespread adoption. Moreover, continuous innovations and rigorous testing must persist before these vehicles can be seamlessly integrated into our daily reality.

Envisioning the future, it's likely that autonomous vehicles will be a key component of smart cities, serving as both a utility and a catalyst for further technological integration. They symbolize a shift towards an automated world that embraces efficiency, safety, and sustainability. Yet, as with any significant transition, collaboration between government, industry, and society will be crucial in navigating the uncertain roads ahead.

Ultimately, the rise of autonomous vehicles is more than just a technological evolution; it is a narrative of human ambition, creativity, and the relentless pursuit of a better future. It challenges us to reconsider our relationship with technology and envision an era where machines and humans coexist harmoniously on the roads of tomorrow.

AI-Driven Transportation Innovations

The transportation landscape stands on the brink of a revolution that bears the unmistakable imprint of artificial intelligence. From swift urban mobility to expansive cross-country logistics, AI's influence is reshaping the ways we move and connect. Recent breakthroughs have elevated transportation technologies to new heights, crafting a vision of the future where efficiency, safety, and accessibility redefine travel. Advancements are not only making journeys faster but also ensuring that they are increasingly seamless and sustainable.

One of the foremost innovations in AI-driven transportation is the optimization of traffic management systems. Cities around the globe are adopting intelligent traffic signals that adjust in real time to changing traffic patterns. These AI systems analyze data from roads, weather conditions, and even spontaneous events to reduce congestion and emissions. With reduced wait times and increased flow efficiency, these systems bring us closer to the dream of smart cities.

Beyond mere traffic control, AI models have been instrumental in revolutionizing public transportation networks. Through predictive analytics, AI can anticipate peak times and adjust schedules dynamically. This optimized scheduling improves public transit operations, reducing unnecessary delays and freeing up resources. Encouraging wider use of public transport subsequently diminishes our carbon footprint and leads to healthier environments and improved urban living conditions.

Examples abound of disruptive technologies that break traditional molds, particularly in freight and logistics. AI-driven platforms integrate with supply chains to forecast demand and recommend shipping routes, taking into account variables like fuel use, weather forecasts, and even geopolitical tensions. By doing so, companies can significantly cut costs and delivery times. These enhancements allow transports to navigate complex global networks as if guided by an unseen hand, deftly sidestepping potential challenges along the way.

Moreover, autonomous drones are poised to redefine last-mile deliveries, automating the process from distribution centers to the customer's doorstep. Coupled with AI, these drones optimize delivery routes, ensuring package security and minimizing delivery times. As drone technology matures, we will likely see the skies bustling with activity, realizing a sci-fi vision that was once purely speculative. It's the dawn of a new logistical horizon where speed meets precision.

AI's role in vehicle-to-everything (V2X) communications can't be overstated. Through this communication, vehicles 'talk' to each other and to infrastructure, enhancing road safety by exchanging critical information such as potential hazards, traffic data, and even warnings about road conditions. These interactions create an interconnected travel ecosystem where every participant contributes to a shared driving intelligence, drastically reducing the scope for human error.

AI doesn't just benefit vehicle-centric modes of transportation; its transformative power extends into non-vehicular avenues as well. Imagine AI-powered traffic flow analysis integrated into city biking plans, encouraging greater safety and efficiency for cyclists. Such systems could recommend optimal routes based on traffic conditions, weather, and even personal preferences, promoting biking as an appealing alternative to traditional urban commuting.

Additionally, there's transformative potential in AI's capacity to personalize user experiences. Future AI systems in vehicles might optimize the cabin environment by adjusting lighting, temperature, and even seat ergonomics, all tailor-fitted to the passenger's preferences. In mass transit, AI can offer curated content or suggest destinations based on past travel behavior or emerging preferences, making public transportation not just efficient, but enjoyable as well.

Moreover, the future of AI-driven transportation innovations rests heavily on the promise of 'green mobility.' AI-driven systems that monitor and optimize energy consumption for both traditional and electric vehicles are pivotal in reducing the transportation sector's environmental footprint. Energy-efficient route planning and dynamic adjustment systems reduce emissions, echoing the broader societal push towards sustainability.

AI in transportation has the potential to overcome significant societal challenges related to accessibility. With AI's capabilities, transportation networks can become more inclusive, offering adaptive solutions for those with disabilities or special needs. By analyzing passenger data, these systems could suggest accessible routes, offer real-time accessibility updates, and integrate with smart urban infrastructures to facilitate unimpeded travel.

Another pivotal factor is AI's role in emergency response and management. Rapid data analysis and real-time response capabilities mean that AI can significantly improve how emergencies, particularly traffic accidents, are handled. By instantaneously rerouting traffic or dispatching emergency services with pinpoint accuracy, AI promises to make roads safer not only for robots but also for humans.

Critically pondering the broader societal ramifications of these advancements, one reflects on the increasing need for strategic regulations and robust ethical frameworks. The integration of AI in transportation raises questions about data privacy, safety standards, and equitable access. Societies will need to carefully mediate the balance between innovation and oversight to ensure these powerful technologies benefit everyone.

In conclusion, the tapestry of AI-driven transportation innovations is being woven with threads of cutting-edge technology, environmental stewardship, and accessibility. The possibilities are vast and varied, promising both transformative efficiency and equitable mobility. As we continue to venture further into this promising future, each innovation reflects our boundless creativity and quest for a more connected world. Looking forward, we see not just vehicles but ecosystems of movement where AI is an invisible yet indispensable partner in the journey toward progress.

Chapter 19:
AI and Augmented Reality

In a world increasingly steeped in digital innovation, the intersection of AI and augmented reality (AR) presents an exhilarating frontier with profound potential. This fusion is redefining how we experience reality, offering new dimensions where our physical and digital lives merge seamlessly. Imagine walking through a city where your view is enhanced by AI-powered visual overlays that provide real-time information, directions, and even immersive storytelling. AI algorithms refine this augmented experience by learning from our interactions, tailoring the digital augmentation to suit our preferences and context. In education and training, AI-driven AR can simulate intricate scenarios, from virtual classrooms that transcend geographical boundaries to hands-on medical procedures for tomorrow's surgeons. As we venture into this augmented future, we face exciting challenges and possibilities, urging us to think deeply about the ways AI can enhance our perception and responsiveness in these enriched virtual spaces. Integrating AI in AR holds transformative potential, nudging us closer to a future where technology uplifts human experience in ways once reserved for the realm of science fiction. Yet, it's essential to tread thoughtfully, navigating ethical landscapes to ensure these advancements align with societal values and aspirations. As innovators and thinkers converge, the horizon for AI-fueled AR beams with promise, inviting us to explore and redefine the boundaries of reality itself.

Enhancing Perceptions with AI

In the rapidly evolving landscape of technology, AI's role in augmented reality (AR) is ushering in a transformation of perception itself. This is not an abstract notion confined to science fiction but a burgeoning reality shaping our interactions with the digital and physical worlds. Augmented reality, powered by artificial intelligence, is poised to redefine how we perceive and engage with reality, blending the virtual with the physical in seamless ways that were previously unimaginable.

At its core, augmented reality aims to overlay computer-generated enhancements on top of real-world environments, offering a composite view that enriches the user's reality rather than replacing it. AI contributes to this vision by enabling systems to understand and interpret the real world accurately. Machine learning algorithms, for instance, can process vast amounts of visual data to identify objects and scenes in real-time, allowing AR applications to deliver contextually aware information and interactions. This enhances user engagement, making the experience more intuitive and personalized.

The integration of AI in AR technology is particularly evident in the improvement of perceptual conciseness and the fidelity of digital overlays. AI algorithms refine how digital content aligns with and reacts to the physical environment, adjusting colors, lighting, and shadows to create a more believable and immersive experience. Consider, for instance, an interior design application that allows users to visualize virtual furniture within their living space. AI not only ensures accurate placement and scaling but also enhances the realism by adapting to ambient light and shadow dynamics, making the virtual elements appear convincingly real.

One of the most groundbreaking applications of AI-enhanced augmented reality lies in its potential to revolutionize education and training. Imagine students exploring historical events not through textbooks but by virtually stepping into them, guided by AI-driven narratives that adapt to their learning pace and style. Such experiences could make learning more engaging and effective, tapping into the natural human inclination for visual and experiential learning.

In the realm of enterprise, AI and AR are reshaping industries ranging from manufacturing to retail. Workers can receive real-time instructions and diagnostics overlaid on machinery, reducing errors and increasing efficiency. In retail, customers can virtually try on clothes or see how products would fit in their homes, all facilitated by AI's ability to personalize interactions and predict preferences based on user behavior and historical data. The fusion of AI with AR is crafting experiences that are not just interactive but predictive, catering to the individual's needs and desires in real-time.

Yet, as with any profound technological shift, the merging of AI and AR invites a host of ethical and societal considerations. The enhanced ability to filter and manipulate perceptions raises questions about authenticity and control. Who decides what digital overlays are permissible in our shared environments, and what are the implications for privacy and consent? These debates will become increasingly pertinent as AI-driven AR becomes a ubiquitous presence in daily life.

Moreover, the capacity for AI to enhance perceptions through AR extends beyond commercial and educational applications into the very fabric of personal and social interaction. By overlaying social data, like facial recognition or emotional analysis, AI could alter how we perceive and relate to one another, for better or worse. There is potential for fostering deeper connections and understanding, but also for reinforcing biases or infringing on personal space.

Nevertheless, the potential for good is vast. AI in AR holds promise for accessibility innovations, providing support and enhancements for disabled individuals. From guiding visually impaired users through public spaces using auditory AR cues to assisting those with learning difficulties through interactive educational tools, the capacity for AI-enhanced AR to improve quality of life is significant.

The path ahead is not without its challenges. As we navigate these advances, careful consideration must be given to the ethical ramifications, ensuring the technology serves humanity's best interests. It is crucial to cultivate an environment where innovation in AI-augmented reality is aligned with robust ethical standards, fostering trust and security for all users.

In conclusion, AI-enhanced AR is more than just an upgrade to our sensory experience; it's a profound leap forward in how we interact with our environment and each other. It possesses the ability to transcend barriers, both physical and cognitive, offering new pathways to knowledge, connection, and creativity. As augmented reality continues to evolve alongside AI, it becomes a canvas where reality and imagination converge, expanding the horizons of human experience in extraordinary ways. Now, more than ever, it's imperative to steer this technological frontier with foresight and responsibility to realize its full potential for the benefit of everyone. The journey ahead promises to be as challenging as it is inspiring—a testament to the enduring human spirit of exploration and innovation.

Integrating AI in Virtual Spaces

As artificial intelligence continues its inexorable march across various facets of our digital existence, one domain stands out for its transformational potential: virtual spaces. The confluence of AI and augmented reality (AR) is reshaping how we perceive, interact with, and ultimately, inhabit these computer-generated environments. With AI's ability to create intelligent and responsive virtual entities, the boundaries of these spaces are constantly being redefined.

Virtual spaces, enhanced with AI, can simulate environments that offer experiences indistinguishable from our physical reality. Imagine walking through a vibrant marketplace bustling with AI-driven avatars, each with its own personality, background, and role to play. This isn't simply science fiction anymore. As AI-driven AR continues to evolve, these spaces become more interactive, intuitive, and immersive. They're no longer just places to visit but arenas to interact, learn, and grow.

The integration of AI in virtual spaces is bringing about a nuanced shift in how users engage with content. Traditional interactions, confined to basic commands and inputs, are being replaced by more dynamic exchanges that rely on natural language processing and machine learning. AI systems can now interpret and respond to our gestures, speech, and even emotions, creating a dialogic interaction that feels more personal and less mechanical. These enhancements allow users an unprecedented level of interaction within these spaces.

Moreover, AI has the potential to transform virtual spaces into personalized environments that adapt to individual needs and preferences. By analyzing user data and behavior, AI can tailor experiences unique to each person, turning virtual spaces into extensions of their personality. This customization offers not only a more engaging experience but also one that aligns closely with users' cognitive and emotional frameworks.

From an educational perspective, the potential applications of AI-driven virtual spaces are boundless. Imagine a classroom that can instantly transform to showcase ancient Rome or take students on a molecular journey through the human body. By providing tangible, interactive experiences, AI can revolutionize learning by catering to diverse learning styles and making education more accessible. Students engage with the material in a more profound way, breaking down complex concepts into comprehensible experiences.

In the business world, the fusion of AI and virtual spaces is leading to innovative ways of conducting meetings, training sessions, and presentations. Virtual offices equipped with AI can function as collaborative environments where geographic and physical constraints dissolve. Team members scattered across the globe can interact in an environment that feels both natural and responsive, with AI managing tasks such as note-taking, scheduling, and even mediating discussions.

One of the most exciting prospects is the development of AI-driven virtual companions—entities that inhabit these spaces and provide companionship, assistance, or entertainment. These AI companions can simulate empathy, offer informed advice, or serve as collaborative partners in creative endeavors. They adapt to users' emotional needs, learning over time to provide better support and companionship. Although the ethical implications of such entities are still being debated, the possibilities for enhancing human experience are immense.

However, with these advancements come challenges and complexities that we need to navigate carefully. The blurring of realities raises important questions about privacy and security, as personal data collected for tailoring experiences could be susceptible to breaches. Furthermore, these immersive environments can also pose psychological risks if individuals begin to spend excessive time in virtual spaces, possibly impacting mental health and social relationships.

There's a need for ethical frameworks and guidelines to govern the integration of AI in virtual spaces. Transparency about data usage, informed consent, and the establishment of safeguards against misuse are essential to ensure these enhancements benefit society as a whole. As AI continues to redefine the parameters of virtual environments, fostering an ecosystem of accountability and responsibility becomes paramount.

Looking ahead, the potential for AI in virtual spaces is enormous. We're just beginning to scratch the surface of what's achievable. As AI specialists, developers, and consumers work collectively, the promise of these environments will be realized, reshaping how we live, work, and play. With AI as our partner in this endeavor, virtual spaces will become rich landscapes of opportunity, creativity, and connection, ushering in a future that's both exciting and unpredictable.

The exploration of such possibilities will undoubtedly continue to inspire innovators and thinkers, propelling us into a new era where the lines between our digital and physical worlds become ever more seamless. On this journey, the symphony of AI and virtual reality will play a core role, guiding us toward unprecedented realms of human achievement and understanding.

Chapter 20:
Preparing the Next Generation

As we stand on the cusp of an AI-driven era, equipping future generations with the right tools becomes paramount. Education systems worldwide must evolve, embracing flexibility and innovation to integrate AI literacy alongside traditional curricula. It's crucial to foster adaptability, encouraging critical thinking and creativity—skills that no algorithm can replicate. Engaging with AI means understanding not just how it functions, but how it can be harnessed responsibly. By promoting interdisciplinary approaches that blend technology, ethics, and humanistic studies, we ensure the rising generation is not just prepared but poised to lead in an uncertain future. Building an environment where young minds are encouraged to question, imagine, and innovate will cultivate a resilient society capable of navigating and shaping the potentialities of AI with wisdom and empathy.

Education for an AI-Driven Future

As we stand on the brink of an AI-driven era, the imperatives for reshaping education are abundant and urgent. The traditional educational models, anchored in rote memorization and standardized testing, face a transformative challenge, demanding a fundamental recalibration of what we learn and how we learn it. Embedded within this evolution is the need to nurture not only technical proficiency but also ethical acuity and creative adaptability. In a future defined by the relentless march of technology, education must foster an environment where students are as inspired by Shakespeare as they are by Python programming.

The integration of artificial intelligence into educational settings promises an unprecedented personalization of learning experiences. Imagine classrooms where AI tailors curricula to fit individual learning paces and styles, identifying strengths and weaknesses with precision. This capability represents a radical shift from the one-size-fits-all model, allowing students to engage deeply with material in ways previously unimaginable. However, this shift must be approached with caution, ensuring that robust pedagogical strategies underpin the use of technology.

Yet, the focus on AI shouldn't supplant the human element. With machines taking over tasks ranging from repetitive to highly complex, human educators' roles are more crucial than ever. Educators must transform into facilitators of learning, guiding students through a curriculum that's not just about absorbing information, but about fostering inquiry, critical thinking, and emotional intelligence. These skills become the "soft power" necessary to thrive in an AI-dominated world.

Incorporating AI technologies in education isn't without its challenges. There are valid concerns about equity and access, particularly in under-resourced schools that may struggle to provide the technological infrastructure required for such advancements. Addressing these disparities is critical, ensuring that every student has the opportunity to benefit from AI-driven educational innovations and that these tools don't inadvertently widen the gap between the haves and the have-nots.

Moreover, as students engage with AI, they also encounter ethical dilemmas that require careful navigation. Developing an understanding of AI ethics and the societal implications of these technologies should be embedded into the curriculum. Students need to learn about the ethical considerations surrounding AI, such as data privacy, algorithmic bias, and the impact of AI decisions on human lives. This awareness fosters a generation of ethically responsible individuals capable of working towards inclusive and fair AI applications.

The future workforce will require skills that are as much about human uniqueness as about technological advancement. Problem-solving abilities, emotional intelligence, and the capacity for ethical reasoning will be as essential as technical skills in programming or data analysis. These future-proof skills become the bedrock upon which students can build careers capable of integrating seamlessly with AI technologies.

Interdisciplinary learning, too, plays an essential role. As AI blurs the lines between computational tasks and creative processes, educational curricula must embrace frameworks that encourage cross-disciplinary scholarship. Innovations often occur at the intersection of traditional fields—combining, for instance, biology with computer science to fuel advancements in healthcare AI. Thus, encouraging students to pursue a breadth of interests and a depth of knowledge in their chosen fields holds significant promise.

Initiatives to re-skill and upskill educators will be equally pivotal. Teachers and professors must be equipped with the knowledge and tools to navigate and impart AI-driven content. Professional development programs focusing on AI literacy will help educators become comfortable with these new technologies, ensuring they can effectively support their students' learning journeys. Continuous learning thus becomes a vital component of an educator's career, mirroring the lifelong learning that is being instilled in students.

Collaborative learning environments must also be fostered, where students can engage in project-based learning alongside their peers globally, tackling real-world problems using AI. Such collaborations can break down geographical barriers, fostering a globally interconnected world view and a shared mission to address planetary challenges. This approach not only enhances technical skills but also cultivates a shared sense of purpose and a broader perspective on global citizenship.

The questions surrounding AI education also bring into focus the necessary partnerships between educational institutions and tech industries. By fostering strong collaborations with companies leading AI research and development, educational institutions can provide students with up-to-date knowledge and skills. These partnerships can result in internship programs and research opportunities that propel students from theoretical understanding to practical applications.

While AI continues to evolve, the educational frameworks discussed serve as the scaffolding to prepare the next generation. This generation isn't just being prepared to survive in an AI-driven world—they are being equipped to drive it, too. The evolution of education must embrace the bold and redefine its paradigms to cultivate a generation ready to contribute meaningfully to society, armed with technological fluency, ethical fortitude, and creative prowess. Education in an AI-driven future holds the potential to be the cornerstone of a world where human and artificial intelligences flourish together, each enhancing the capabilities of the other in a shared pursuit of progress and innovation.

Cultivating Future-Proof Skills

In a world that's increasingly shaped by artificial intelligence, cultivating future-proof skills is more crucial than ever. As AI technologies integrate further into every facet of our lives, the skills we nurture today will define our capacity to navigate and thrive in tomorrow's world. This transformation is not only technological but also deeply human, requiring a blend of technical know-how and enduring cognitive abilities.

Historically, educational systems have focused heavily on rote learning and standardized testing. However, as machines increasingly take over tasks that involve repetitive precision, there's a pressing need to pivot towards fostering creativity, critical thinking, and emotional intelligence—skills that machines can't replicate just yet. This shift demands a rethink of our educational paradigms, emphasizing adaptive learning environments that nurture curiosity and innovation.

Adaptability is emerging as a cornerstone of future-proof skills. In a rapidly changing landscape, the ability to learn, unlearn, and relearn is invaluable. This doesn't just mean technical skills or programming languages that are hot today but might be forgotten tomorrow. Instead, it's about cultivating a mindset willing to embrace uncertainty and change. As futurist Alvin Toffler once posited, the literate of the 21st century are not those who can read and write but those who can learn, unlearn, and relearn.

The integration of AI into various sectors necessitates an education framework that prepares individuals to work alongside these intelligent systems. It's crucial to understand not just how to use AI tools but to question their outputs and ethical implications critically. Students should be equipped with the skills to design, audit, and judge these systems, ensuring they can contribute meaningfully and responsibly in AI-driven contexts.

This emphasis on ethical AI literacy is key. As AI systems grow more autonomous, the lines between human decision-making and machine logic blur, making it imperative to understand AI's societal impacts thoroughly. By instilling a strong foundation in ethics and responsibility early on, we prepare a generation not just to create intelligent systems but to do so conscientiously.

Moreover, interdisciplinary approaches to learning are gaining traction. The future doesn't belong to specialists but to "T-shaped" individuals—those with deep knowledge in one area and a broad understanding across multiple disciplines. This diversity of skills enables them to connect ideas from various fields, fostering innovation and holistic problem-solving. In practice, this could mean combining insights from fields like psychology with computer science or using design thinking principles to enhance AI technologies.

Soft skills, often undervalued in traditional technical education, will also serve as differentiators in an AI-driven job market. Emotional intelligence, communication skills, and teamwork are increasingly vital as work environments become more collaborative and client-focused. AI may excel in data processing and pattern recognition, but understanding human emotions and interactions remains uniquely human.

Additionally, nurturing an entrepreneurial spirit can empower individuals to carve out new niches and opportunities in an AI-augmented world. Encouraging risk-taking, resilience, and innovative thinking prepares students to not just fit into existing roles but to create and redefine them. As AI continues to disrupt industries, those who can envision new possibilities will lead the charge in transformation.

There's also the practical aspect of technical literacy. While not everyone will become a data scientist or machine learning engineer, a working understanding of data analysis, coding principles, and AI mechanisms will be useful. These are the tools of the future workplace, and familiarity with them can enhance one's ability to leverage AI effectively, whether you're in finance, healthcare, or the arts.

The cultivation of future-proof skills extends beyond formal education and into lifelong learning. In a world where the half-life of skills is continually shrinking, the curiosity to seek new knowledge and the humility to update one's competencies are crucial. Lifelong learning ecosystems, supported by technology, such as online courses and AI-driven personalized learning paths, provide platforms for ongoing growth.

Internships and real-world experiences play a significant role in skill cultivation too. By immersing individuals in actual work environments, they gain access to dynamic learning experiences, engage with diverse team dynamics, and witness firsthand how AI tools are applied across industries. This synergy of theoretical knowledge and practical application forms a rounded understanding that classrooms alone may not offer.

Ultimately, as we prepare the next generation, it's essential to develop a narrative that integrates technology seamlessly with human values. This means fostering a worldview that doesn't see AI as a threat but as a tool to enhance human potential, a platform for innovation, and a catalyst for achieving societal goals. It's about harmonizing the binary logic of machines with the nuanced complexities of human life.

The road to a future where human skills complement, rather than compete with, AI is paved with intentional education, ethical foresight, and an openness to perpetual learning. By focusing on adaptability, interdisciplinary knowledge, ethical literacy, and emotional intelligence, we empower individuals to not just survive but to thrive in the ever-evolving tapestry of our AI-enhanced future.

Chapter 21:
AI Ethics and Responsibility

As artificial intelligence continues shaping our world, the call for ethics and responsibility in its development grows increasingly urgent. The evolution of AI forces us to examine what it means to be accountable in an interconnected global society, where machines make decisions that affect millions of lives. Implementing responsible AI practices isn't just about preventing harm; it's about fostering trust, ensuring fairness, and preserving human dignity amidst rapid technological change. We face challenges that demand a commitment to designing systems transcending mere efficiency, drawing from diverse ethical frameworks to guide AI's integration into everyday life. As we stand on the brink of unprecedented societal shifts, the responsibility to harness AI for the greater good becomes a defining task for policymakers, technologists, and citizens alike. It's a collective endeavor that asks us to balance innovation with moral foresight, shaping AI to enhance our shared human experience rather than diminish it.

Accountability in AI Design

In the realm of artificial intelligence, accountability is more than a mere ethical consideration; it is a necessity that underpins the trust society places in these technologies. As AI systems increasingly influence critical aspects of our lives, the question of who is accountable for their decisions becomes paramount. Whether it's a self-driving car making a split-second decision or an AI-assisted diagnostic tool in healthcare, determining responsibility in the event of failure is not just a technical challenge but also a moral imperative.

To understand accountability in AI design, we must first examine the complex web of stakeholders involved. These systems are rarely the product of a single entity. Developers, engineers, data scientists, businesses, and even policy-makers play roles in creating and deploying AI technologies. This networked approach requires a clear delineation of responsibility to ensure that AI operates within ethical boundaries and societal norms. Each stakeholder must own their part in this technological tapestry, from the initial data fed into an algorithm to the final user interaction.

Accountability in AI design necessitates transparency in system operations. AI models, particularly those leveraging deep learning, often function as black boxes, providing little insight into their decision-making processes. This opacity poses a significant challenge in assigning accountability. If we can't trace how an AI arrived at a particular conclusion, holding any party accountable becomes difficult. Transparent AI, supported by explainable AI models, is crucial for ensuring that users and designers alike understand a system's behavior.

A case in point can be seen in AI applications within law enforcement. Predictive policing algorithms, designed to allocate resources effectively, must be transparent to ensure they do not perpetuate biases or unjust practices. If left unchecked, these technologies could unfairly target certain communities. Ensuring accountability through transparency can prevent misuse and promote fairness, enhancing public trust in AI systems.

Incorporating ethics into AI from the ground up is essential for building accountable systems. Just as an architect considers the safety of a building's design, AI developers should integrate ethical frameworks during the design phase. This approach can anticipate potential ethical dilemmas and mitigate risks before they arise. A proactive stance on ethics fosters a culture of accountability, where AI is aligned with human values and societal goals.

Moreover, the principle of responsibility-sharing should be applied across the AI lifecycle. AI accountability isn't only about addressing failures post-deployment; it involves a comprehensive approach that encompasses the entire development process. Identifying and articulating responsibilities at each stage—from data collection and pre-processing to algorithmic tuning and consumer deployment—ensures that every phase is subject to oversight. Consequently, potential issues are addressed collaboratively, and their impact is minimized.

Legal frameworks and industry standards also play pivotal roles in fostering accountability. Governments and international bodies must work together to develop regulations that hold companies and developers accountable without stifling innovation. Standardized guidelines can ensure that AI systems are built and operated responsibly across jurisdictions. Harmonizing legislation across borders is crucial in our interconnected world, where AI technologies transcend national limits faster than laws can adapt.

Accountability is also about empowerment. Users need to be equipped with knowledge and tools to understand and challenge AI decisions. Empowerment through education ensures that individuals are aware of their rights and the mechanisms available to hold AI systems accountable. As AI becomes ubiquitous, a digitally literate society can provide a check against potential abuses, ensuring AI serves the collective good.

However, challenges persist. As AI systems evolve, keeping ethical standards and accountability frameworks up to date becomes challenging. Technologies like neural networks can autonomously adapt and learn, creating scenarios where the original developers may not predict the system's decisions. Continuous updates to ethical guidelines and accountability measures are necessary to reflect technological advancements and societal shifts.

Collaborations between academia, industry, and government are essential to advance accountability in AI design. By pooling resources and expertise, these sectors can develop comprehensive strategies to address the multi-faceted nature of AI accountability. Sharing best practices and lessons learned from past implementations can drive progress in creating more reliable and trustworthy AI systems.

Consider the potential societal benefits of accountable AI systems. When designers and developers prioritize accountability, AI can support human goals in powerful ways. For example, accountable AI in healthcare can lead to profound improvements in patient outcomes by ensuring unbiased diagnosis and treatment recommendations. Similarly, in education, systems designed with accountability can provide personalized learning experiences that respect and adapt to individual needs without compromising privacy or fairness.

Looking forward, the goal should be to embed accountability into the very DNA of AI design. As AI systems become increasingly autonomous, the challenge of accountability might seem to grow. However, with a commitment to ethical design principles, clear lines of responsibility, and robust legal frameworks, we can harness AI's full potential while safeguarding human values.

In closing, accountability in AI design is a fundamental component of ethical AI development. It requires a concerted effort from diverse stakeholders, integrating transparency, ethical guidelines, and legal frameworks to ensure that AI technologies are aligned with societal norms and values. By addressing accountability proactively, we can lay the foundation for AI systems that enhance human life and preserve our collective well-being.

Implementing Responsible AI Practices

In the quest to harness the vast potential of artificial intelligence, ensuring its responsible deployment is no longer a choice but an imperative. The rise of AI technologies presents both incredible opportunities and significant ethical challenges. How we choose to navigate these challenges today will determine the impact of AI on society for generations. Implementing responsible AI practices means fostering development and deployment methods that align with ethical norms and promote the well-being of all individuals.

The first step in implementing responsible AI involves a commitment to transparency. AI systems, often characterized by their complexity, must be designed to provide insight into their decision-making processes. This includes not just high-level explanations but also access to detailed justifications of how decisions are reached. Such transparency is key to cultivating trust amongst users and stakeholders, ensuring they can understand, scrutinize, and if necessary, challenge AI-driven outcomes.

Accountability is another cornerstone of responsible AI implementation. With AI systems often making decisions that significantly impact lives, knowing who is responsible when things go wrong is critical. Clear guidelines and structures must be put in place to designate accountability not only for the outcomes generated by AI but also for the data on which these systems depend and the algorithms that power them. This requires organizations to undertake due diligence in AI system development and deployment, especially regarding their potential societal impact.

Moreover, ensuring fairness in AI systems is crucial. AI applications must avoid promoting biases or exacerbating existing inequalities. This requires developers to be vigilant from the outset, addressing biases in training data, algorithmic design, and overall system functionality. Fairness in AI can be promoted through regular audits, leveraging diverse and representative datasets, and implementing inclusive design practices that consider the diverse demographic and social contexts of potential users.

Data privacy also forms a critical pillar of responsible AI practices. AI systems thrive on data, yet the use of sensitive personal information raises substantial privacy concerns. Organizations must establish robust safeguards to protect personal data at every operational stage. This includes employing methods like data anonymization and employing stringent data security protocols. Users should always be informed about how their data is being used and possess the autonomy to control its flow according to their preferences.

Ethical AI deployment cannot ignore the significance of human oversight. While autonomous systems are an alluring prospect, maintaining a human-in-the-loop approach ensures that critical decisions, especially those with moral or ethical ramifications, remain under human control. This maintains a balance where AI complements human capabilities without displacing the essential judgment and empathy that humans bring to decision-making processes.

Another integral aspect of responsible AI involves fostering inclusivity in AI research and development. Bringing together diverse voices within AI teams helps to build systems that reflect and respect community heterogeneity. Diverse teams are more likely to foresee and mitigate adverse outcomes, thus creating more robust and beneficial AI technologies. Cooperation across international borders can further enrich this inclusivity, fostering global dialogue that acknowledges various cultural, ethical, and legal perspectives.

Equally significant is the need for continuous education and awareness. As AI technologies evolve, so too must our understanding of their capabilities and implications. Organizations should invest in training programs that equip employees, stakeholders, and the general public with the knowledge necessary to engage with AI responsibly. Such endeavors not only deepen understanding but also empower individuals to participate constructively in conversations about AI's role in society.

Finally, exit strategies for AI systems need careful consideration. While AI provides unparalleled benefits, systems should be designed with the capacity for deactivation or rollback in case they pose unforeseen risks or adverse effects. These strategies ensure that AI remains a tool that serves humanity's interests rather than one that operates beyond human control or understanding.

In conclusion, implementing responsible AI practices is a complex, multifaceted endeavor. It requires a commitment from all stakeholders—developers, businesses, governments, and society at large—to prioritize ethical considerations throughout an AI system's lifecycle. Only then can we fully realize a future where AI acts as a powerful ally to humanity, enhancing our lives and addressing some of our most pressing global challenges while upholding fundamental ethical standards. By embedding responsibility within our AI technologies, we lay the groundwork for a more equitable and sustainable future.

Chapter 22:
Visionaries and Thought Leaders

In the rapidly evolving landscape of artificial intelligence, visionaries and thought leaders stand as the navigators of uncharted waters, daring to reshape the future with bold imaginations and innovative ideas. They blend profound understanding with indomitable curiosity, steering the dialogue around AI's potential in the next half-century. These pioneers—spanning technologists, ethicists, and futurists—challenge the conventions by envisioning AI's role in solving global crises, enhancing human capability, and reimagining societal structures. Their perspectives serve as beacons, offering guidance amid the fog of uncertainty and the excitement of possibility. By drawing insights from various disciplines, these leaders challenge us to envision a world where AI not only complements human life but fundamentally enriches it. As we lean into the future, their dynamic and diverse contributions light the path towards achieving a transformative alliance between humanity and technology.

Perspectives Shaping AI's Future

The future of artificial intelligence is a landscape shaped by a multitude of perspectives, each one contributing to a vision that will define the relationship between machines and humanity for decades to come. At the heart of these perspectives are the visionaries and thought leaders who, through diverse backgrounds and insights, provide a roadmap for navigating the complexities of AI technology.

Consider the technologists, scientists, and ethicists who each bring distinct viewpoints to the table. They grapple with questions that challenge the very essence of what it means to create machines capable of independent thought. The debates among them aren't just technical but philosophical, exploring existential inquiries about intelligence, consciousness, and ethics. Their collective wisdom not only propels innovation but also anchors it in a framework of responsibility.

Technology visionaries often emphasize the transformative potential of AI, viewing it as a tool that could solve some of humanity's most intractable problems. From accelerating scientific research to addressing crucial challenges in fields like healthcare and climate change, these leaders are tasked with steering AI toward a future that enhances human potential rather than restricts it. They push for developments in AI that could enable real-time translation of languages, lead to personal assistants that understand users' nuances, and open new frontiers in space exploration.

However, the optimism of these innovations must be balanced by cautionary insights from ethicists who warn of the social consequences if such technologies are not guided by ethical principles. These voices caution against unchecked AI development that could lead to surveillance states, exacerbate inequalities, or make autonomous decisions devoid of human empathy. Their role in shaping AI's future is paramount, as they spearhead frameworks that aim to humanize technology, ensuring it aligns with societal values.

Meanwhile, an interdisciplinary approach from thought leaders in sociology and cultural studies offers an understanding of how AI reshapes personal and collective identities. They examine the impacts on cultural norms, community structures, and societal interactions, considering both the integration and augmentation of human capabilities by machines. As AI continues to permeate daily life, these scholars advocate for the preservation of cultural diversity and individuality amidst technological homogenization.

Entrepreneurs and business leaders bring yet another perspective, focusing on the economic imperatives of AI. They seek to harness the power of AI to drive innovation, reduce operational costs, and create new markets. While the immediate focus may be on profit and efficiency, influential leaders in this space also stress the need for corporate responsibility in AI applications, promoting fair employment practices and long-term sustainability.

Such a plethora of perspectives would be incomplete without input from policymakers and legal experts who contend with crafting legislation that keeps pace with rapid technological advancements. Their efforts aim to strike a fine balance between fostering innovation and safeguarding public interests, laying the groundwork for regulatory frameworks that ensure ethical AI development. By considering public discourse, they endeavor to represent varied societal interests and values in policy formation.

Furthermore, educational leaders hope to reshape the paradigm of future generations' engagement with AI. They advocate for curriculum development that not only prepares students with technical skills but also instills an understanding of ethical implications and a capacity for critical thinking. Their influence extends beyond education, as they often provide thought leadership in navigating AI's social complexities, advising industries and governments on how to foster a more inclusive and equitable digital society.

In summary, the perspectives shaping AI's future are as multifaceted as the technology itself. These varied viewpoints are essential in crafting a multifaceted, resilient approach to AI development that incorporates technological advancement with ethical considerations, cultural understanding, economic opportunity, and legal structure. By continuously engaging these diverse perspectives, we can aspire to create an AI-driven world where technology is a source of empowerment rather than division, steering humanity toward a common good inspired by collective wisdom.

Influencers in AI Innovation

In the expansive arena of artificial intelligence, where ideas rapidly ascend and transform industries, a select group of individuals stands at the forefront, shaping the trajectory of AI innovation. These are the influencers—luminaries whose work, thoughts, and discoveries continually propel artificial intelligence toward new horizons. They're not just researchers or developers; they're visionaries who see what others can't, adopting interdisciplinary insights to break new ground.

Each influencer carries a unique perspective and expertise, yet common themes permeate their work: a relentless pursuit of knowledge and a dedication to ethical considerations in technological advancement. As AI's role in society becomes increasingly significant, the contributions of these leaders are essential not only for technological progress but for ensuring that innovation is aligned with human values and needs.

The people recognized as influencers in AI innovation often come from diverse backgrounds, embodying multidisciplinary approaches to problem-solving. One cannot overlook the transformative influence of computer scientists who pioneered early algorithms and machine learning principles that laid the groundwork for contemporary AI. These individuals have been instrumental in shifting AI from theoretical concepts to practical applications that can be found in nearly every industry today.

Alongside computer scientists are experts from fields like cognitive science, neuroscience, and even philosophy. Their contributions bring depth to AI systems, infusing them with nuances of human cognition and decision-making processes. This blending of knowledge domains not only enriches AI technologies but ensures they are better equipped to learn, adapt, and function in complex human-centered environments.

In the realm of deep learning, researchers have unlocked pathways that were previously unimaginable. Their groundbreaking work on neural networks has enabled machines to perform tasks such as image and speech recognition with remarkable accuracy. By continually pushing the envelope, they've opened doors for AI to perceive and interpret the world more like humans do, bridging gaps between human and machine interactions.

Equally transformative are the entrepreneurs who have embodied the spirit of innovation by successfully translating research into scalable AI solutions. These individuals have founded and led enterprises that leverage AI for solving real-world challenges, making significant impacts across sectors such as healthcare, financial services, and education. Their vision has not only stimulated economic growth but also improved quality of life, underscoring AI's potential for societal benefit.

Each AI innovator also contends with ethical decisions that accompany technological advancement. Many have advocated for robust frameworks that regulate AI's development and deployment, ensuring that technological capabilities do not outpace ethical considerations. Their leadership in this area is essential as society grapples with AI's role in privacy, security, and human rights.

Furthermore, these influencers extend their reach beyond academia and industry circles. They engage in public discourse, openly sharing their ideas, challenges, and solutions. By doing so, they foster an environment where knowledge is shared, and innovation thrives through collaboration. Their influence extends to policy-making, where they help shape legislation that governs the use and development of AI technologies.

The impact of AI influencers is not confined to immediate technological advancement. By inspiring a new generation of thinkers and creators, they yield a lasting legacy. Through mentoring, public speaking, and academic contributions, they cultivate environments that nurture talent and encourage bold explorations in AI research and applications.

As AI continues to evolve, the role of these influencers becomes ever more vital. Their ability to see beyond the present, envision future possibilities, and navigate complexities within both technological and ethical realms positions them as pivotal architects of our AI-driven future. Their collective efforts ensure that the trajectory of AI development remains a tool for good, emphasizing innovation that is inclusive, equitable, and sustainable.

Their stories and achievements remind us that while technology can tremendously advance our capabilities, it is the human element—characterized by imagination, compassion, and responsibility—that guides innovation toward truly transformative outcomes. In celebrating these influencers, we recognize the profound interplay between technology and humanity, underscoring the need for conscientious leaders to steer AI's monumental impact on our world.

Chapter 23:
The Limits of AI

As we delve into the capabilities and boundaries of artificial intelligence, it's crucial to recognize that, despite its impressive advancements, AI remains bound by inherent constraints. While it excels in processing vast amounts of data, performing complex calculations, and even mimicking certain aspects of human behavior, AI lacks the nuanced understanding and emotional intelligence that defines human experience. The absence of genuine creativity, intuition, and empathy in AI systems highlights a fundamental limitation: their operations are grounded in algorithms and datasets, devoid of true consciousness or awareness. Moreover, AI's dependency on human-designed frameworks and its struggle with tasks requiring common sense or adaptability to unforeseen situations further illustrate these confines. Thus, as we continue to innovate and incorporate AI into various facets of life, acknowledging its limitations will be essential for harnessing its full potential while avoiding over-reliance on its capabilities. This balanced approach will not only advance AI responsibly but also safeguard against unmet expectations and ethical pitfalls as we journey into a future increasingly shaped by intelligent machines.

Understanding AI's Capabilities

As we delve into the augmented realm of artificial intelligence, it's essential to grasp the scope of its capabilities. The technological landscape has profoundly shifted with AI's introduction, yet its full potential still eludes complete understanding. What we know is that AI thrives in environments where data is abundant, and tasks can be predictably structured. The prowess of AI shines particularly bright where pattern recognition is crucial, far surpassing human capabilities in the speed and scale of data processing.

Machine learning, a subset of AI, has been remarkably successful in emulating certain cognitive tasks. These include natural language processing, image recognition, and through advancements in deep learning, even intricate decision-making processes. The more data AI systems consume, the more refined their outputs become, showcasing a remarkable ability to learn and adapt. This adaptability, however, is both a strength and a limitation, for AI relies heavily on the data provided to it, which can sometimes lead to unforeseen biases.

Take, for instance, the domain of healthcare. AI systems now assist in predicting patient outcomes and diagnosing diseases with impressive accuracy. These systems analyze a multitude of variables that might be too overwhelming for human doctors alone. Yet here, we witness AI's dependency on data quality and comprehensiveness. An AI model trained on a limited or biased dataset may produce skewed results, highlighting an inherent weakness: AI cannot transcend its training environment without external intervention or data.

The versatility of AI is notable in autonomous systems too. Self-driving vehicles navigate complex environments by synthesizing data from a host of sensors in real-time. They merge mapping data with on-the-ground observations to drive safely. While their perception frameworks are continually improving, they still struggle in uncommon situations where behaviour deviates from the norm, necessitating human intervention. A critical barrier for AI in unpredictable environments remains its challenge in understanding and responding to context in comparative ways a human does.

The creative domains stretch another frontier of AI's capabilities. Machine-generated art and music push the boundaries of what we traditionally define as creative work, challenging our notions of originality and inspiration. However, AI's outputs are always traceable back to existing datasets, repurposing rather than innovating from scratch. This capability to generate art brings excitement, yet simultaneously questions AI's limits regarding authentic creativity.

Equally remarkable is AI's ability to enhance human-computer interactions, seen in personal assistants like Siri and Alexa. These systems enable more natural communications and efficient task management. But they still falter with nuanced human emotions and complex sentiments, underscoring the symbiotic need for human-like intuition and empathy that AI cannot yet replicate.

Moreover, AI's computational ability in areas like finance, where algorithms can predict market trends or automate transactional decisions, has revolutionized the sector. Simultaneously, quick reliance on AI in high-stakes environments amplifies the risk of systemic failures, if these systems fail to anticipate rare, volatile events, as they often lack comprehensive models for unprecedented scenarios.

Despite these notable strengths, AI faces considerable constraints. Emotional intelligence, ethical judgements, and abstract thought are arenas where humans retain a definitive edge. AI's rationale is bound by the logic codified into it, lacking moral viewpoints unless predefined by its creators. As AI systems lack consciousness, their decision-making remains, in essence, a reflection of human input rather than an independent entity demonstrating true understanding.

In summary, while it's tempting to herald AI as revolutionary, it serves primarily as a powerful tool orchestrated by human hands. The utility of AI spans numerous sectors, often serving as a complement to human work rather than an outright replacement. As we continue to elevate AI's capabilities through innovative research, understanding its current limitations is crucial. These limitations offer a lens through which we can imagine future advancements responsibly, integrating AI into society with clear-eyed expectations and grounded hopes.

Boundaries Yet to Be Overcome

Artificial Intelligence (AI) has undeniably transformed many aspects of our lives, from revolutionizing industries to reshaping cultural norms. Yet, despite its remarkable advances, AI still faces several significant boundaries that challenge its ultimate potential. These boundaries are not just technical, but also ethical, societal, and philosophical. Understanding these limits can serve as a guiding compass for navigating the complex landscape of AI's future.

One of the fundamental boundaries AI struggles with is the concept of true understanding versus task-specific abilities. Unlike humans, who possess a holistic understanding of their surroundings, AI is typically confined to the parameters set by its design. Deep learning systems, while adept at pattern recognition, do not genuinely understand the content they process. This lack of comprehension leads to issues when AI systems encounter data or scenarios outside their training sets. The inability to generalize knowledge without specific programming is a significant hurdle that researchers continue to grapple with, raising concerns about AI's effectiveness in dynamic, real-world situations.

Moreover, the aspiration to create AI with consciousness or self-awareness remains an elusive goal. Consciousness, the quintessential human trait characterized by subjective experience, is something AI cannot replicate with current methodologies. Philosophers and technologists debate whether consciousness can ever be achieved with computational systems, questioning whether it is necessary or even desirable for AI. The pursuit of consciousness in AI not only involves technical challenges but also ethical dilemmas, as it raises questions about rights, responsibilities, and the moral status of intelligent systems.

Ethical considerations present another boundary that AI must confront. The ability of AI systems to make decisions, especially in high-stakes settings like healthcare or autonomous vehicles, necessitates frameworks that guide ethical decision-making processes. Yet, designing these frameworks is fraught with complexity. Ethical guidelines must account for diverse cultural norms, subjective moral philosophies, and unpredictable real-world variables. The lack of universally accepted ethical standards remains a hindrance to the widespread deployment of AI technologies, with risk-averse sectors waiting for clearer guidance and protections against possible misuse or unintended consequences.

Data privacy is another critical boundary AI has yet to overcome. The reliance on large datasets for training AI models poses substantial risks to individual privacy. Balancing the need for data to enhance AI capabilities with the protection of personal information is a dilemma that has yet to be fully addressed. As AI technologies become more integrated into daily life, ensuring robust data privacy measures without stifling innovation is a challenge that echoes across tech companies and regulatory bodies worldwide.

There are also intrinsic technical limitations associated with current AI methodologies. Machine learning models require substantial amounts of data and computational power, which can be a significant barrier to entry for smaller entities or under-resourced regions. Moreover, the high energy consumption required for training large models contradicts global efforts towards sustainability. Developing more energy-efficient AI systems that do not sacrifice performance is critical for making AI more accessible and environmentally conscious.

Additionally, language and cultural understanding still pose significant barriers. While AI translation services have improved, they often miss contextual subtleties essential for genuine cross-cultural communication. Idiomatic expressions, cultural references, and nuances can lead AI to mistakes that may cause miscommunication or offense. Enhancing AI's ability to understand and appropriately interact across different cultures and languages is crucial for its future integration into a globally connected world.

AI's impact on the workforce also reveals boundaries yet to be overcome. While AI offers the promise of efficiency and the automation of routine tasks, it also threatens existing job structures, creating the need for a redefined relationship between humans and machines. Workers must adapt to work alongside AI, developing skills that complement and refine AI capabilities. How we manage the transition for different sectors, ensuring economic stability while promoting innovation, is a pressing concern.

The legal frameworks surrounding AI lag behind technological advances. Regulatory and legislative bodies struggle to keep pace with rapid AI development, resulting in a patchwork of policies that vary widely across jurisdictions. This inconsistency can hinder innovation and adoption due to unpredictable legal environments. Global cooperation and harmonization of AI laws could offer solutions, but achieving consensus among nations with different priorities and perspectives is no small task.

Furthermore, biases embedded in AI systems remain a formidable challenge. Bias can enter AI models through skewed training data or flawed algorithmic expressions, leading to decisions that can perpetuate social inequalities. Addressing bias involves not only refining algorithms but also ensuring diversity in the data, the teams developing the AI, and the objectives guiding their work. Despite recognized advancements, biased outcomes in AI continue to undermine its credibility and acceptance, necessitating ongoing vigilance and correction.

The trust deficit between AI systems and users is another boundary yet to be overcome. For AI to be truly transformative, it must earn the trust of its users through transparency, reliability, and accountability. The opaque nature of many machine learning models stands in stark contrast to the need for explainability, especially where decisions have significant impacts on human lives. Developing AI that can transparently justify its decision-making processes will be crucial for building trust and widespread acceptance.

Despite these challenges, the boundaries AI faces offer opportunities for innovation and improvement. They require interdisciplinary collaboration, blending insights from computer science, ethics, sociology, law, and philosophy. While overcoming these boundaries is no simple feat, it is crucial for realizing AI's potential to support and enhance human capabilities, fostering a future where AI acts as a partner rather than a competitor.

As we navigate the evolving landscape of AI, these boundaries serve as guideposts. They remind us that advancing AI is not just about technological prowess, but also about reflection, responsibility, and resilience. By addressing these challenges with foresight and determination, we can unlock AI's full potential, creating a future where AI serves the greater good. In overcoming these boundaries, we engage not just in the development of technology, but in the crafting of a more equitable, informed, and empathetic world.

Chapter 24:
Living in Harmony with AI

In a world where artificial intelligence increasingly influences our lives, living in harmony with these technologies requires both wisdom and adaptability. As AI systems become more embedded in our social fabric, it's essential to view them not merely as tools but as evolving partners in our journey toward a more connected and efficient society. This collaboration calls for conscious integration, where human values and AI's capabilities align to enrich our daily experiences. By fostering open dialogues and developing adaptable frameworks, we can ensure that AI complements human creativity and empathy. The path forward is about balancing control and trust, enabling AI to enhance our quality of life without compromising our fundamental rights. As stewards of this transformative relationship, we must remain vigilant, open-minded, and ever willing to learn, ensuring that AI remains a force for good—shaping futures that resonate with our highest aspirations.

Navigating Coexistence with Technology

The burgeoning relationship between humans and artificial intelligence demands a delicate balance, one that allows for the seamless integration of technology into our lives without compromising fundamental human values. As AI continues to evolve at an unprecedented pace, living in harmony with these systems requires a nuanced understanding of their potential and limitations, as well as proactive measures to ensure their adoption enhances rather than hinder our collective well-being.

Central to achieving a harmonious coexistence with AI is the concept of symbiosis, where both humans and technology benefit from their interplay. This dynamic requires an intentional design of AI systems that are not only efficient and capable but also aligned with human needs and ethical standards. As we have seen throughout history with past technological revolutions, the path to harmonious integration is fraught with both opportunities and challenges. The potential to augment human capabilities with AI is immense, offering solutions to complex problems, from healthcare diagnostics to environmental conservation.

However, navigating this coexistence is not without its challenges. One pressing concern is ensuring equitable access to AI technologies. Without deliberate efforts to bridge the digital divide, advancements in AI could exacerbate existing inequalities, leaving marginalized communities further behind. Therefore, policymakers, technologists, and civil societies must collaborate to create frameworks that promote inclusivity and fairness in the dissemination of AI innovations.

This collaboration can manifest in various forms, from deploying AI to tackle local community challenges to developing user-friendly AI applications that cater to diverse populations. By prioritizing accessibility, we can ensure that AI serves as an equalizer, providing opportunities for empowerment across different socioeconomic strata.

Addressing the ethical dimensions of AI is equally crucial. As AI systems make increasingly autonomous decisions, embedding robust ethical standards becomes paramount. The decisions made by AI, especially in sensitive areas like healthcare and criminal justice, carry significant moral weight. Researchers and ethicists are called upon to craft AI algorithms that not only fulfill functional criteria but also adhere to ethical guidelines that reflect society's values and principles.

This task requires ongoing dialogue among stakeholders, including governments, private sector leaders, and the general public. Transparency in AI development and deployment processes fosters trust and allows for democratic oversight, ensuring that the path to technological integration respects human rights and individual freedoms.

In envisioning a future where AI and humans coexist peacefully, education plays a pivotal role. Educating the public about AI's capabilities and limitations not only demystifies the technology but also empowers individuals to engage with it more meaningfully. From a young age, incorporating AI literacy into educational curriculums can equip future generations with the skills necessary to navigate and shape an AI-driven world responsibly.

This educational effort extends beyond traditional schooling. Ongoing learning opportunities for adults, including workshops and online courses, can help bridge knowledge gaps as AI technologies evolve. By fostering a culture of continuous learning, we ensure that society adapts alongside technological advancements, minimizing disruptions and maximizing benefits.

Economic considerations also play a significant role in negotiating our coexistence with AI. The economic landscape is continuously being reshaped by AI, with automation threatening certain job sectors while creating novel opportunities in others. Proactively managing this transition by developing reskilling programs and supporting workforce mobility is vital to mitigate adverse impacts and capitalize on new economic prospects.

Moreover, AI has the potential to drive innovation in ways previously unimaginable. Industries can leverage AI to streamline operations, reduce waste, and enhance creativity, ultimately contributing to economic growth and sustainability. To harness these benefits, it is imperative to cultivate an entrepreneurial environment that encourages experimentation and rewards innovation.

Lastly, cultural shifts in perceptions of AI are necessary to foster a harmonious future. Fear and skepticism often accompany discussions about AI, fueled by dystopian narratives and misunderstanding. Engaging in open, evidence-based conversations about AI's role in society helps dispel myths and cultivate a mindset receptive to the transformative possibilities AI offers.

By embracing a forward-thinking and action-oriented approach to AI integration, society can navigate the complexities of living alongside advanced technology. This journey requires resilience, adaptability, and a shared vision of a future where AI amplifies human potential, reflecting our collective aspirations for progress and well-being.

Collaborative Futures with AI

The concept of collaboration between humans and artificial intelligence is not merely a vision of the future; it is an evolving paradigm that is quickly becoming a foundational element in many aspects of our lives. AI's role isn't just as a tool to automate repetitive tasks or analyze vast sets of data—it is emerging as a genuine partner in creative and decision-making processes. As we delve into what it means to live collaboratively with AI, we find opportunities for innovation as well as challenges that will require careful navigation.

At the heart of any successful collaboration is communication. This statement holds as much truth for human partnerships as it does for interactions between humans and AI. Developing AI systems that understand and adapt to human intentions and emotions is crucial to creating effective partnerships. One exciting area of progress is natural language processing (NLP), which allows AI to understand and generate human-like text. With ongoing advancements, NLP can serve as the bridge between humans and machines, making interactions more intuitive and meaningful.

Collaborative AI systems can assist in various fields, offering unique insights that might not be immediately obvious to human counterparts. For instance, in the realm of scientific research, AI can analyze patterns within complex datasets, providing researchers with novel hypotheses to explore. This collaborative effort accelerates the pace of discovery by sifting through vast amounts of information faster than what would be feasible manually, allowing scientists to focus more on experimentation and innovation.

Creativity, often considered quintessentially human, is another frontier where AI collaboration is redefining boundaries. From music composition to visual arts, AI collaborates with artists, not to usurp but to expand the possibilities of creative expression. By processing and learning from countless works, AI can suggest new styles or techniques, offering artists fresh perspectives and challenging traditional paradigms. This dynamic dance between human creativity and machine capability paves the way for new art forms yet unimagined.

The workplace is another domain ripe for transformation through AI collaboration. Beyond automation, AI systems can augment human skills, offering support in complex cognitive tasks. Imagine a world where professionals across industries have AI partners that not only automate mundane tasks but also assist in strategic planning, providing risk assessments or market forecasts that allow for more informed decision-making. This kind of collaboration doesn't replace human intuition and leadership—it enhances them.

One might wonder how AI collaboration will influence human relationships and societal structures. The ripple effects of AI-human collaboration extend beyond technological advancement; they touch upon cultural evolution as well. As AI becomes more integrated into our daily routines, it reshapes traditional roles and identities. Embracing these changes requires a willingness to redefine what it means to work, create, and even socialize. It is an opportunity to expand our cultural repertoire, blending innovation with tradition.

Nevertheless, the path to harmonious AI-human collaboration is not without hurdles. Ethical considerations loom large in this landscape. Who owns the intellectual outputs of a human-AI partnership? How do we ensure transparency in AI decision-making processes, particularly in critical areas like healthcare or finance? These are questions that demand reflection and decisive action, guiding the development of robust frameworks that balance innovation with ethical considerations.

Furthermore, trust is a cornerstone of any successful collaboration. Building trustworthy AI requires rigorous testing and validation, ensuring that systems operate reliably and are free of biases. Trust is also about transparency; users should be able to understand AI's decision-making processes, knowing when and how these systems reach their conclusions. Initiating dialogues between developers, ethicists, and users will be key to building trust and ensuring that AI serves humanity's best interests.

The educational sphere plays a pivotal role in preparing future generations for collaborations with AI. As AI becomes an ever-present fixture in society, equipping individuals with the knowledge to work effectively alongside AI is crucial. This means not only understanding AI's capabilities and limitations but also fostering skills such as critical thinking and creativity, which are inherently human and essential in a world influenced by AI innovations.

Ultimately, the future of AI-human collaboration hinges on flexibility and adaptability. As AI technologies evolve, so must our approaches toward integration and collaboration. The ability to anticipate changes and adapt to them will define successful ventures in this shared future. It calls for open-mindedness, a willingness to challenge preconceived notions, and a commitment to continuous learning and development.

Collaborating with AI represents more than just a technological advancement; it symbolizes an opportunity to redefine our potential as a society. By embracing the collaborative capabilities of AI, we can tackle some of the world's most pressing challenges, from climate change to healthcare disparities. In building this future, we must be guided by principles that prioritize both technological progress and human values, ensuring that AI serves to amplify human potential rather than diminish it.

In conclusion, the journey toward a collaborative future with AI is as much about technological advancement as it is about human evolution. It requires a holistic understanding of how AI can complement human abilities, while safeguarding the values that define us. As we stand at the threshold of this transformation, we must choose to view AI not as an existential threat but as an ally, harnessing its capabilities to build a more connected and innovative world.

Chapter 25:
Imagining AI 50 Years From Now

In envisioning the world a half-century hence, the trajectory of artificial intelligence offers a landscape both familiar and unfathomably transformed. As we stand at this precipice, pondering our future with AI, the challenge is to thread the line between optimism and conscientious forethought. Imagine AI systems not just as tools but as partners in combating global issues like climate change, or catalysts in revolutionizing education and healthcare. While the seeds of these changes are visible today, the potential outcomes in 50 years may redefine our very understanding of human achievement and companionship. AI could enable breakthroughs in quantum computing, bioengineering, and even interstellar exploration, turning sci-fi dreams into reality. Yet, this future also demands a sober evaluation of ethical and societal implications—how do we ensure AI serves humanity without eroding essential human values or freedoms? Our preparedness will be tested, requiring adaptive policies, robust ethical frameworks, and a steadfast commitment to equity across all facets of AI deployment. In this contemplation, the essence of AI lies not merely in technological advancement but in its capacity to reshape our shared future, offering endless possibilities as long as we're ready to guide it responsibly.

Predictions and Projections

As we look ahead fifty years, the landscape of artificial intelligence stands poised for breathtaking transformations. With the rapid advancements we've witnessed in recent decades, it's curious to consider just how far AI might take us. Will AI operate in every facet of daily life? Can it elevate human capabilities or potentially even reshape our existence? The trajectory of AI's evolution suggests a future filled with profound possibilities and inevitable challenges.

We can expect that AI's integration into our lives will deepen, likely becoming as indispensable as electricity is today. Future AI systems might not only understand human language and emotions with incredible accuracy but could also anticipate our needs and desires before we express them. Imagine virtual assistants that know when you need a pick-me-up cappuccino, or an AI helping you navigate complex social scenarios at the push of a button. These are not wild fantasies; they're potential realities based on current trends.

One of the most exciting projections is AI's potential to solve some of the world's most pressing issues. Consider climate change—a challenge that requires complex data analysis and rapid, global action. AI could optimize energy consumption, predict environmental changes, and even implement solutions autonomously. Though the notion seems ambitious, AI's role in addressing such global concerns cannot be overstated. By 2073, sustainable AI-driven technologies might dominate efforts in environmental conservation and rehabilitation.

In the realm of healthcare, AI could revolutionize medical diagnostics and personalized treatment plans. Picture AI systems capable of processing a lifetime of medical data for every person, offering precise diagnosis and treatment tailored to each individual. This would mark a significant shift from reactive to proactive healthcare. By enhancing decision-making processes, AI could extend average human lifespans and improve quality of life on an unprecedented scale.

Education will likely undergo a seismic shift, too. With AI's capacity to personalize learning experiences, traditional educational models might be transformed or even rendered obsolete. Each student's journey could be tailored to their unique needs, ambitions, and learning styles, with AI tutors available around the clock. While educators might focus more on fostering creativity and critical thinking, AI could alleviate much of the repetitive, administrative burden.

Yet, the possibilities AI presents are tempered with substantial ethical and practical considerations. As AI systems grow in sophistication, questions around data privacy, security, and human autonomy will become increasingly paramount. How societies agree to responsibly integrate AI while safeguarding individual freedoms and rights will define much of the next fifty years. Developing robust AI ethics frameworks will be crucial.

Moreover, the global race for AI leadership might intensify. Nations will compete not just for technological supremacy but also for influence over international AI standards and policies. Collaborative global governance could emerge, but geopolitical tensions might also rise. Leveraging AI for peace and collaborative innovation presents both an opportunity and a challenge for future generations.

The future of work will undoubtedly be affected as well. While automation may displace certain jobs, it's also likely to create new roles that we can't yet envision. Reskilling and lifelong learning could form the backbone of professional life, requiring workers and governments to adapt continuously. AI might empower workers to innovate and excel, transforming workplaces into hubs of creativity and technological synergy.

We also anticipate profound impacts on human relationships and society. AI companions might become more prevalent, possibly serving as friends, confidants, or caretakers. This raises important questions about the nature of human interactions and the essence of communication. The boundaries between human and machine might blur, challenging us to rethink identity and community.

Notably, we'll face the philosophical and existential query of AI and consciousness. If AI systems become sophisticated enough to exhibit apparent consciousness, what rights, if any, should they hold? Such discussions could redefine our understanding of intelligence, consciousness, and ethical responsibility.

Technologically, the outer limits of AI's capabilities are still being explored. Might we create machines that outperform human intelligence in every regard? These artificial entities, sometimes referred to as superintelligence, could hold the potential to monumentally advance or be perilous if not carefully controlled. Preparing our regulatory and ethical frameworks for these eventualities should be a priority.

In conclusion, the narrative around AI fifty years from now is one that's still being written. The predictions and projections are tantalizing, yet they serve as reminders of AI's transformative power. The interplay of technological innovation, ethical considerations, and socio-political frameworks will shape whether AI becomes a force for good or a challenge to navigate. As we embark on this journey, the commitment to harness AI responsibly, ensuring it benefits all humanity, must steadfastly guide our endeavors.

Preparing for Uncertain Changes

As we peer into the future and envision artificial intelligence fifty years from now, an undeniable theme emerges: change. The very nature of AI—with its swift advancements and boundless potential—mandates

175

that societies, economies, and individuals brace for transformations that are difficult to predict with precision. But while the exact contours of the future may remain fuzzy, preparing for uncertainty is not only prudent but essential. This means developing strategies and mindsets capable of adapting to the unforeseen, all while harnessing the transformative power of AI for human benefit.

In the world of AI, change isn't just an update or a tweak; it's a seismic shift that can disrupt industries and redefine daily life. Fifty years down the line, AI might be rewriting the rules in every sector imaginable. Whether it's how we work, communicate, or even perceive reality, each aspect of life may experience a fundamental transformation. To prepare, we need to adopt a dual perspective: one eye fixed on current trends and innovations, and the other gazing forward to anticipate what's next. It's about building a bridge between the present and the potential future, allowing us to traverse the unknown with confidence.

Adaptability is the keystone in this process. Individuals, organizations, and governments alike must cultivate flexibility in decision-making, operations, and thought processes. For instance, today's educational systems can no longer afford to be static. Infusing curricula with skills like critical thinking, creativity, and digital literacy is vital to equip the next generation for roles that don't yet exist. Such forward-thinking education fosters resilience, enabling future workers to navigate and thrive amidst continual technological evolution.

Moreover, as AI continues to mature, ethical considerations will grow in complexity. Decisions made today about the deployment and control of AI will reverberate through paths untrodden. Thus, integrating ethical frameworks into AI development and implementation is not just a choice—it's an obligation. They function as guiding lights, ensuring that progress doesn't outpace societal trust or moral standards. By focusing on ethics, we embrace a proactive stance, ready to manage the moral implications and unintended consequences that AI could pose in the future.

Equally crucial is fostering public dialogue concerning AI's trajectory and its societal impacts. Engaging communities in discussions about technological advancement democratizes the conversation, ensuring a diversity of voices shapes the policies and practices governing AI. Such inclusivity not only cultivates a shared vision but also identifies potential pitfalls before they become entrenched challenges. If society is to prepare effectively for unknown changes, it must do so as a collective, with every voice contributing to the chorus.

Significant transformation also demands robust policy frameworks that support innovation while safeguarding public interest. Policymakers must operate with foresight, crafting regulations that are as dynamic as the technologies they govern. These laws and guidelines must balance innovation with protection, allowing flexibility where needed but drawing clear lines to prevent misuse or harm. By constructing a policy landscape that evolves alongside AI, we create a cushion against uncertainty, providing both security and opportunity for growth.

Similarly, industries must reimagine their paradigms, shifting from static to agile models. Businesses that embrace AI as a partner rather than a simple tool will find themselves at the forefront of innovation. By investing in research and development, fostering partnerships with AI experts, and remaining open to reinvention, organizations can not only adapt to change but drive it. Industries that successfully integrate AI can expect to unlock new levels of efficiency, creativity, and profitability, ensuring their relevance in a rapidly changing world.

On a global scale, international collaboration and competition will play a pivotal role in shaping AI's future. Nations must navigate the tension between leveraging AI for national advantage and collaborating on global issues like climate change, healthcare, and security. Establishing international consensus on AI standards and ethics will be paramount to harnessing its benefits while curtailing risks. By engaging in cooperative efforts, countries can share knowledge and innovations, ensuring AI strengthens global resilience, not just individual coffers.

As we prepare for AI's uncertain changes, personal growth and mindset shifts are equally important. Individuals should embrace lifelong learning as a norm rather than an exception, constantly updating skills to remain relevant in a tech-driven world. Resilience, adaptability, and a willingness to embrace change can transform uncertainty into opportunity, allowing individuals to ride the wave of AI advancements rather than be swamped by them.

Ultimately, preparing for the unpredictable future of AI is a multidimensional endeavor. It demands a balance of anticipation and reactivity, where strategies are both deliberate and flexible, ethics are robust yet adaptable, and innovation coexists with regulation. By engaging in comprehensive and proactive preparation, we can stand ready to meet the opportunities and challenges AI will bring fifty years from now, ushering in an era not just of technological evolution but of enriched human potential.

Conclusion

As we stand on the precipice of a future intertwined with artificial intelligence, it's crucial to reflect on the journey we've traversed and the road that lies ahead. Through the exploration of AI's foundations, societal impacts, and potential innovations, we've glimpsed a world that's both exciting and daunting. This book has attempted to capture the vast landscape of AI's possibilities and challenges, providing an informed perspective on the profound transformations that await us.

The advancements in AI technology have been nothing short of revolutionary. New breakthroughs continue to expand our understanding of what's possible, making it clear that AI isn't just a tool—it's becoming a fundamental aspect of our social and economic fabric. Yet, with great potential comes the responsibility to ensure that AI's integration into society adheres to ethical principles that promote equity and justice. As AI permeates various sectors, including healthcare, education, and governance, it raises critical questions about privacy, security, and ethical implications.

AI's integration into the workforce and its effects on cultural norms illustrate the profound societal shifts underway. While concerns about job displacement are legitimate, AI also brings opportunities for new kinds of work and efficiencies that were previously unimaginable. Moreover, AI's ability to personalize and enhance learning experiences in education shows promise for fostering an adaptable and skilled workforce prepared for the demands of the future.

The intersection of AI and ethics remains a contentious yet vital area of dialogue. Developing robust ethical frameworks and engaging in philosophical debates about AI rights and accountability are necessary steps as we integrate AI further into our lives. In parallel, discussions about AI legislation and government use of AI technologies highlight the need for comprehensive policies that can address the myriad issues AI presents.

On the environmental front, AI holds the potential to revolutionize climate change strategies and drive sustainability efforts. Yet, these innovations must be balanced with a keen awareness of the environmental footprint and potential challenges posed by developing and deploying AI technologies on a global scale.

Despite the massive potential of AI, understanding its limitations is just as crucial. While imagination often runs wild with possibilities, maintaining a grounded perspective on AI's actual capabilities ensures that we don't oversell its potential or rely too heavily on yet-to-be-perfected technologies. Moving forward, fostering collaboration between AI and humanity will be essential.

In business, AI's transformative effect is indisputable, reshaping models and enhancing customer experience. Businesses are encouraged to harness AI strategically, ensuring that they remain competitive while blending innovation with ethical considerations. Similarly, AI's creative capacities present new frontiers in art and communication, challenging and expanding our understanding of collaboration and expression.

Not to forget, the global perspective on AI adoption underscores the importance of international collaboration to nurture AI development responsibly and equitably across diverse socio-economic landscapes. Competing on the frontiers of AI innovation, nations must strike a balance between competition and cooperation.

Beyond Tomorrow: The Future of AI and Humanity

The philosophical and moral questions raised by AI challenge our conception of consciousness and what it means to be human in an AI-infused world. These discussions compel us to consider our role in shaping AI's trajectory and the legacy we wish to leave for future generations.

In contemplating AI's future, particularly over the next fifty years, speculation suggests a tapestry of unpredictable changes. While AI advancements are inevitable, our ability to adapt, guide, and harness these changes will determine whether the future will be one of unprecedented opportunity or unforeseen challenges.

Ultimately, living in harmony with AI hinges on our willingness to engage with technology with an open mind and moral compass, fostering a future where AI and humanity coexist productively. The integration of AI will define our era, and it is our responsibility to steer its impact toward the collective good.

This book hopes to have provided a thoughtful exploration of AI's potential, highlighting the dynamic landscape of challenges and opportunities. The path forward demands vigilance, creativity, and collaboration, ensuring that AI evolves thoughtfully and ethically within our global community.

Appendix A: Appendix

The appendix serves as a supplementary resource to the main body of this book, offering reference materials, clarifications, and a deeper dive into some of the concepts discussed throughout the text. It's designed to be a practical guide for those who wish to expand their understanding or who might seek additional information on certain topics.

1. Further Reading and Resources

Given the rapidly evolving nature of artificial intelligence, staying informed about the latest research, trends, and developments is crucial. The following is a compilation of recommended books, articles, journals, and online courses that provide diverse perspectives on AI's present and future.

Books exploring the foundational theories and modern advancements in AI.

Articles and white papers published by thought leaders in the AI community.

Academic journals featuring peer-reviewed research on AI advancements and their implications.

Online courses offering in-depth understanding and certification in various AI fields.

2. Glossary of Terms

This glossary contains definitions and explanations of key terms and concepts that appear throughout the book, helping readers to better understand the technical language associated with AI.

Artificial General Intelligence (AGI): A form of AI that possesses the ability to understand, learn, and apply knowledge across a variety of tasks as a human does.

Neural Networks: A series of algorithms designed to mimic the way the human brain operates, often used in pattern recognition and machine learning tasks.

Machine Learning (ML): A subset of AI focused on the development of algorithms that allow computers to learn from and make predictions based on data.

3. Ethical Guidelines

The integration of AI into daily life raises numerous ethical questions, addressed in this appendix by setting out key guidelines for developing and deploying AI technologies responsibly. These guidelines align with the ethical principles discussed earlier in the book.

Ensure transparency in AI models and algorithms.

Prioritize privacy and data protection.

Promote fairness and avoid algorithmic biases.

Facilitate accountability in AI decision-making processes.

4. Frequently Asked Questions

This section addresses some of the most common inquiries about AI that might not have been fully covered in the main chapters, offering concise and direct answers to satisfy a reader's curiosity.

How can AI impact the future job market?

AI is likely to transform the job market by automating routine tasks, changing the skills that are in demand, and creating new job categories that do not exist today.

What is the role of ethics in AI development?

Ethics play a critical role in ensuring that AI systems are designed and used in a way that is beneficial, fair, and unbiased, safeguarding against misuse and negative impacts.

The appendix is not just a conclusion but rather an open invitation for ongoing exploration and discourse, offering the necessary tools and insights to engage in the vibrant narrative of artificial intelligence and its boundless potential. Through this journey, readers are better equipped to navigate the complexities of an AI-augmented future, enriched with understanding and prudence.

www.ingramcontent.com/pod-product-compliance
Lightning Source LLC
Chambersburg PA
CBHW021142070326
40689CB00043B/977